NEW ORLEANS
Classic
DESSERTS

NEW ORLEANS *Classic* DESSERTS

Recipes from Favorite Restaurants

KIT WOHL

PELICAN PUBLISHING COMPANY

GRETNA 2007

First printing, January 2007
Second printing, April 2007
Third printing, August 2007

The word "Pelican" and the depiction of a pelican are trademarks
of Pelican Publishing Company, Inc., and are registered in the
U.S. Patent and Trademark Office.

ISBN 9781589804449

Edited by Lloyd Dobyns, Brigit Binns, and Michele Vine

Printed in Korea
Published by Pelican Publishing Company, Inc.
1000 Burmaster Street, Gretna, Louisiana 70053

FOR MY SWEET. BILLY, MY HUSBAND.

Contents

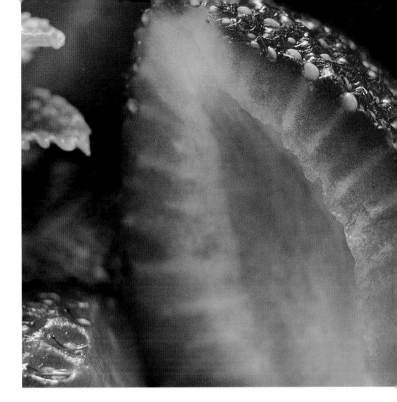

INTRODUCTION

"STRESSED SPELLED BACKWARDS IS DESSERTS. COINCIDENCE? I THINK NOT!"

~Author Unknown

There's a reason we call it The Big Easy. We don't like stress. We do like desserts. In fact, nothing is more New Orleans than a sweet memory.

We Orleanians celebrate at lunch and dinner—and we crown our celebrations. An important meal isn't complete without the grand finale of a classic dessert. Even an unimportant meal (if there is such a thing) demands some dessert.

Not that you need a meal to celebrate dessert.

During the '50s and '60s, there was a patisserie on Royal Street in the French Quarter. The most delectable array of confections would wink at me through glass cases; it was delicious agony to settle on just one. After I'd make my choice, I'd take it, paired with a cup of hot chocolate or café au lait, to the lush courtyard behind the shop. An exquisite, almost secret sweetness. Under the trees. In the middle of the morning. Or afternoon.

That too is New Orleans.

This book is a collection of some of my favorite dessert recipes from world-renowned New Orleans restaurants and chefs, plus some from cherished, talented friends. They include the simple glory of Sister Mary's Pecan Pralines, Emeril's stunning Banana Cream Pie, Arnaud's Creme Brûlée, Brennan's flaming Bananas Foster, Bread Puddings, or the elegant grace of Crozier's Floating Island.

As you know, New Orleans' culinary heritage is based on its Spanish, French, Italian, Caribbean, African, Indian and German roots. Each group brought something to the party, and we know we are the better for it, which is why I've also included the stories and legends behind the recipes.

In New Orleans, we're so proud of our heritage we eat it every day.

The thing about desserts is this: Not only do they make people happy, they allow cooks to strut their stuff. Jewel-toned fruits, bright glazes and garnishes offer a colorful palette for creativity.

Done right, a New Orleans dessert will bring you to your knees.

Of course, there's a difference between what a professional makes and making your own. Pastry chefs, bakers, confectioners, chocolatières, and pastissiers are royalty in the culinary world, and, of necessity, a bunch of persnickety perfectionists.

Who else would invest so much talent and time—and so many precious ingredients—in order to create a small masterpiece that might be destined to disappear in a single bite?

No matter. These recipes aren't written for the professional, although they may make you look like one. Each recipe has been home-kitchen tested by real people who are not chefs in real life.

A recipe straight from a chef or restaurant without testing is illegal around here. Chef's have experience, knowledge, and special tricks. We want you to be happy, look good, and duplicate simply and relatively easily a famous recipe.

Dessert-making is much easier when following a few basic rules.

Arrange a time when there are no other distractions. Read the recipe carefully. Read the recipe again. Gather the ingredients. Avoid substitutions. Assemble the equipment and (this is important) take the time to measure everything into separate bowls and containers before cooking anything.

Chefs refer to this procedure as preparing the mise en place. The practice—and the phrase—are easy to remember if you think of it as having your mess in place. Sound complicated? It isn't. Trust me on this one.

Stressed? No, desserts.

Now turn on the music, pour yourself a glass of something, and begin making your own sweet New Orleans memories.

– Kit Wohl

CAKES & PIES

One holiday season not long ago, a dear friend (and co-cooking enthusiast) and I decided to celebrate by producing desserts. We are good cooks, we assured each other, although rarely had our sweets received requests for second helpings, except for her pies.

We selected easy recipes, just in case.

An astonishing mess with dreadful results ended the day. The neighborhood children refused our offerings. Her ever-hungry golden retriever, Ollie, also declined.

It was time to rethink baking.

It was only through restaurateur friends, and access to their pastry chefs, that I finally grasped the differences between cooking a meal and making a dessert.

Their lessons resulted in these incredible, edible confections. It was a got it! moment for someone who measures by the handful or a splash. "Pay attention, follow the instructions, buy good ingredients, and use the right equipment," they commanded. "You can cook with the utensils in the kitchen drawer, but you can't make desserts. To make desserts, you either do it right, or you don't do it. No kidding."

I listened.

CHEF EMERIL LAGASSE
BANANA CREAM PIE

Like most virtuoso performances, the applause following a banana cream pie presentation is heady acknowledgement. Prepare your response. Practice saying "It is nothing," modestly with a smile in your voice.

YIELD: 9-INCH PIE

4 cups	heavy whipping cream	1	graham cracker crust (recipe on page 91)
1-1/2 cups	whole milk		
1-1/2 cups plus 2 teaspoons	granulated sugar	3 pounds (about 9)	ripe but firm bananas, peeled and cut cross-wise into 1/2-inch slices
1	vanilla bean, halved length-wise, seeds and pods	1/2 teaspoon	vanilla extract
2 large	eggs	garnish	caramel sauce
3 large	egg yolks		chocolate sauce
1/2 cup	cornstarch		(recipes on page 90)

Split the vanilla bean lengthwise and scrape the seeds from the pod.

Combine 2 cups of the cream, the milk, 1/2 cup of the sugar, the vanilla bean, and the vanilla seeds in a large heavy saucepan and bring to a gentle boil over medium heat, whisking to dissolve the sugar. Remove from the heat.

Combine the eggs, egg yolks, cornstarch, and 1 cup of the sugar in a medium bowl and whisk until pale yellow. Slowly add 1 cup of the hot cream into the egg yolk mixture, whisking constantly until smooth. Gradually add the egg mixture to the hot cream and whisk well to combine.

Bring to a simmer, stirring constantly with a heavy wooden spoon, and cook until the mixture thickens, about 5 minutes. (The pastry cream may separate slightly; if so, remove from the heat and beat with an electric mixer until smooth.) Press through a fine-mesh strainer into a clean bowl. Cover with plastic wrap, pressing it directly against the surface to prevent a skin from forming. Refrigerate until well chilled, approximately 4 hours.

To assemble, spread 1/2 cup of the pastry cream over the bottom of the prepared crust, smoothing it with the back of a large spoon or rubber spatula. Arrange enough banana slices (not quite one-third) in a tight tiled pattern over the custard, pressing them down with your hands to pack them firmly.

Repeat to build a second layer, using another 3/4 cup of the pastry cream and enough bananas to cover it. For the third layer, spread 3/4 cup pastry cream over the bananas and top with remaining bananas, starting 1 inch from the outer edge and working toward the center. Spread the remaining pastry cream evenly over the bananas, covering them completely to prevent discoloration. Cover with plastic wrap and chill for at least 4 hours, or overnight.

In a medium bowl, whip the remaining 2 cups cream until soft peaks form. Add the remaining 2 teaspoons of sugar and the vanilla extract and whip until stiff peaks form.

With a sharp knife dipped in hot water, cut the pie into 10 slices. Transfer the slices to dessert plates. Fill a pastry bag with the whipped cream and pipe some onto each slice. (Alternatively, spread the whipped cream evenly over the pie before cutting.)

Drizzle each slice with the slightly warmed Caramel Sauce, or Chocolate Sauce. Sprinkle with chocolate shavings and confectioners' sugar and serve. (Recipes for crust, caramel sauce, and chocolate sauce are on pages 90-91.)

Recipe with permission from *Emeril's New New Orleans Cooking.*

Chef Emeril Lagasse has shaken the culinary world, resulting in increased recognition for New Orleans, and our legacy of great restaurants. While his restaurant empire ranges across the country, his background, and home base operations here are matters of local pride. I've always wanted to call it home plate but that's a matter of opinion. He's given back to the city much more than great food, and is a hometown hero.

His tour as executive chef with Commander's Palace gave him an appetite for adventure. When he christened Emeril's the restaurant world rocked while he rolled. The Food Network program "Emeril Live" has taught cooks everywhere to view food as entertainment, no matter where it is prepared.

In New Orleans, Emeril's, Delmonico, and NOLA showcase his talent.

Chef Emeril's take on Banana Cream Pie is all about entertaining guests.

PASTA FROLLA (Pie Crust)

7 ounces	unsalted butter, softened
1/2 cup	granulated sugar
pinch	salt
2 large	egg yolks
1/2 teaspoon	vanilla extract
2 1/3 cups plus 2 tablespoons	all-purpose flour

In a large bowl, cream together the butter, sugar, and salt. Beat in the egg yolks one at a time, beating until the first is fully incorporated before adding the second, and scraping down the sides of the bowl. Add the vanilla. Fold in the flour, mixing until just combined. Chill the dough for 20 minutes before rolling it out. This step is crucial for handling such a fragile dough; otherwise it will fall apart. However, it is easily patched with small bits of pastry.

On a floured surface, roll out into an 11-inch circle and very carefully place in a 9-inch tart pan. Patch cracks, and holes as necessary with the trimmings. Chill for 20 to 40 minutes to prevent shrinking.

Once the dough is firm, bake it "blind" in a 350°F oven with pie weights (pennies, beans or rice in an oven-bake bag). Baking blind means baking only the pie crust without the filling. When the edges just start to turn golden, remove the pie weights, and bake 5 to 10 minutes longer, until the crust is a little dried out.

CHEF DONALD LINK
BROWN BUTTER BANANA TARTLET

Chef Donald Link presides over his tiny Warehouse District restaurant, Herbsaint, named after the New Orleans liqueur. There Creole and Cajun specialties take star turns on his menu. He draws from other cuisines in an international juxtaposition of products, flavors, and techniques. Desserts such as his Brown Butter Banana Tartlet reflect Louisiana's sugar cane fields.

He burnished his talent as sous chef to Chef Susan Spicer at Bayona, her restaurant. As partners she and Link opened Herbsaint, a kicky Warehouse District bistro frequented by locals and visiting fans.

Link has also opened Cochon Restaurant, a purely Cajun-hearted establishment. It highlights his southern Louisiana origins, including cochon de lait, roast pig prepared in a wood-burning oven. Country fare is the menu's backbone.

Both restaurants have received national acclaim, awards, and recognition for culinary excellence. Forbes magazine named Chef Link a Top Ten Chef to Watch and New Orleans magazine called him Chef of the Year.

YIELD: 9-INCH TARTLET

12 ounces	unsalted butter		1	cinnamon stick, broken
1/4	vanilla bean, scraped (split the vanilla bean lengthwise and using a spoon, scrape the seeds for use)		6 large	egg yolks
			1-1/2 cups	granulated sugar
			6 tablespoons	all-purpose flour
			2	ripe bananas, sliced 1/2 inch thick, divided (reserve half the slices to garnish the tart top)

In a heavy-bottomed saucepan, combine the butter, vanilla bean, and cinnamon. Place over low heat. When the butter has melted, let simmer gently until the butter solids have turned brown (the darker, the better the flavor, but be very careful not to let them burn). Strain through a chinois or other fine mesh strainer. In a bowl, whisk the egg yolks, and sugar together until fluffy, and pale. Slowly drizzle in the butter, and then fold in the flour. Cover the custard, and chill for several hours or overnight.

Once the pie shell has been baked, layer the bananas on the bottom of the shell, and fill the tart with about 4 to 5 ice cream scoops of the brown butter custard. Do not overfill, or the custard will spill over during baking. Continue baking until the custard turns golden, approximately 20 to 25 minutes.

Caramelize the banana slices for the top of the pie by placing them on a baking sheet covered with aluminum foil. Sprinkle the slices with granulated sugar. Using a cook's butane torch, lightly toast the sugar-coated banana slices until the sugar melts, and turns golden brown. Garnish the pie.

An optional method is to melt 1 tablespoon of unsalted butter with 3 tablespoons of granulated sugar, and dip the banana slices into the caramel.

Tip: Bury the leftover vanilla bean husk in a jar of sugar. It will add flavor for future use.

CHEF ROBERT BARKER
CAFÉ BRÛLOT PUDDING CAKE

Ovenproof demitasse cups and spoons find their way to the dessert table when filled with a single mixture that ingeniously separates during baking into cake on the top and custard on the bottom. It looks like a tiny soufflé and tastes like New Orleans famous Café Brûlot, laced with cognac, cinnamon, cloves, lemon, and orange. It's a spectacular surprise for your guests and for you–it's simple.

YIELD: 12 DEMITASSE CUPS OR 6 SERVINGS IN CUSTARD CUPS

1-1/2 cups	whole milk, scalded		1/2 teaspoon	lemon zest
1 cup	sugar		1 teaspoon	orange zest
1/4 cup	flour		1 tablespoon	fresh lemon juice
1/4 teaspoon	cinnamon		2 tablespoons	fresh orange juice
1/4 teaspoon	ground cloves		2 tablespoons	cognac
pinch	salt		4 large	eggs, separated
2 tablespoons	unsalted butter, melted		4 tablespoons	strong espresso

Preheat oven to 325°F.

In a small saucepan, scald the milk. Set it aside.

In a large bowl, combine the sugar, flour, cinnamon, cloves, salt, melted butter, lemon and orange zest, lemon and orange juice, and cognac. Stir together to blend. This is the base mixture.

In another bowl, beat the egg yolks; add the scalded milk slowly, stirring constantly.

Whisk the egg mixture into the base mixture. In a perfectly clean bowl, beat or whisk the egg whites to stiff peaks. Fold into the base mixture.

Pour into 12 ovenproof demitasse cups, 6 buttered custard cups or a buttered 1-quart casserole dish. Arrange cups or casserole in a larger baking pan, and carefully pour in approximately 1 inch of hot water. Bake demitasse cups for 25 to 30 minutes; custard cups for 35 minutes; a casserole dish for 45 minutes. Insert a toothpick into the dish to check if the cake is done, and the custard is firm. It should not jiggle.

Garnish with an espresso stick or curl of orange or lemon peel, and dust with cinnamon. Break the crust with a demitasse spoon, and pour 1/2 teaspoon of cognac or an orange-flavored liqueur into the wound. It might gild the lily, but then again, it is a sensational flourish.

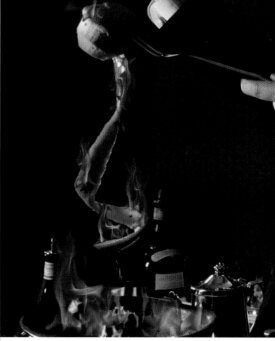

© Photograph Paul Rico

After graduating from New Orleans' Delgado Culinary Arts program, Chef Robert Barker spent his first three years in an apprenticeship tour of the city's most distinctive restaurants.

Delgado's respected program is modeled after the European apprenticeship system. A student rotates through accredited restaurants, and attends class on off-kitchen days. Three years of practical experience with pay and plus academics make it one of the country's finest schools. Restaurants compete for these students.

Barker completed his apprenticeship at Arnaud's, then joined Wolfgang Puck in Los Angeles for what he calls his MBA in cooking. He followed up as executive sous-chef with Emeril Lagasse in New Orleans, and later earned his toque—although he wears a baseball cap—as an executive chef.

Barker relishes creating new ways of presenting flavor combinations, and cooking is his passion. "Food," he says, "is my focus. Our family gets together for holidays. The continuous two-or three-day food fest begins with visits to the farmer's markets and ends with soups and gumbos from the leftovers. That's what it is all about."

Restaurants evolve through the decades and Delmonico is no exception. The century-old New Orleans institution was acquired by Emeril Lagasse when the former proprietors retired.

It is a restaurant with a past, as Emeril puts it. Delmonico received a first class face-lift and all the accoutrements necessary to satisfy a gracious lady's longing. The menu received the same treatment, sparked by Emeril and his creative culinary team.

The original Delmonico opened in New York in 1837, and permitted use of the name in New Orleans in 1895.

Streetcars rattled past Delmonico when it opened, and they continue to pass in front of the restaurant located at an uptown corner of St. Charles Avenue.

DELMONICO
CHOCOLATE PIE

Delmonico former proprietors, Angie Brown and Rose Dietrich, served a comfortable, homey chocolate pie that was light and rich. It was a tribute to the heartiness of their menu.

As chocolate pies go, it was a benchmark, and completely satisfying. It may be dressed up with chocolate curls, meringue, and other decorative flourishes but somehow that seems to take away from it's honest simplicity.

The chocolate pie is not on the new menu but Emeril's specialties replace it with updated versions of exquisite desserts. If you were a fan of the chocolate pie, now it may be made at home.

YIELD: 8-INCH PIE

2 tablespoons	cocoa powder		2 cups	half-and-half
2-1/2 tablespoons	corn starch		6 ounces	semi-sweet chocolate chips, melted
2/3 cup	granulated sugar		1 ounce	unsweetened chocolate, melted
1/8 teaspoon	salt		1 tablespoon	softened butter
1 cup	heavy whipping cream		2 teaspoons	pure vanilla extract
3 large	egg yolks, whisked		1	pie crust, baked blind

Preheat oven to 450°F.

Bake 1 pie crust according to the recipe on page 83 or use a prepared pie crust.

In a medium heavy-bottomed saucepan, add the sifted cornstarch, sugar, cocoa powder, and salt. Slowly stir in the heavy whipping cream. Place pan over medium high heat, and temper the egg yolks by adding the well beaten egg yolks to the mixture very slowly while whipping very quickly. Tempering means do not add the eggs too quickly or the eggs will cook. Add the half-and-half, followed by the melted chocolate, stirring carefully but well. The chocolates will form little dark bits but will melt as mixture heats.

Bring mixture to a boil, stirring slowly but constantly using a wooden spoon. Do NOT use a whisk. (The vigorous whisking will apparently break down the starch molecules and cause a runny mess). When it begins to boil, reduce heat to low, and slowly boil for 2 more minutes.

Strain mixture through a fine sieve into a large bowl. Immediately add the butter and vanilla, stir well to incorporate, pour into a baked pie crust, and place a piece of plastic wrap over surface to prevent a skin from forming while you make the meringue.

Preheat oven to 375°F.

Assemble meringue quickly. The recipe is on page 25. The key to a firm pie filling is putting the meringue on as warm a filling as possible. Spread meringue to edges of pie crust, since it shrinks during baking, and a seal is important.

Place pie in the oven to brown the meringue for approximately 10 to 15 minutes and watch it carefully. If the edges of the pie crust are browning too quickly, cover with a ribbon of aluminum foil. An alternative is to brown the meringue topping on the pie with a butane kitchen torch.

NOTE: Whipped cream may be used as a substitute for the meringue. After baking, pipe or pile meringue on in swirls, once the pie has chilled, just before serving.

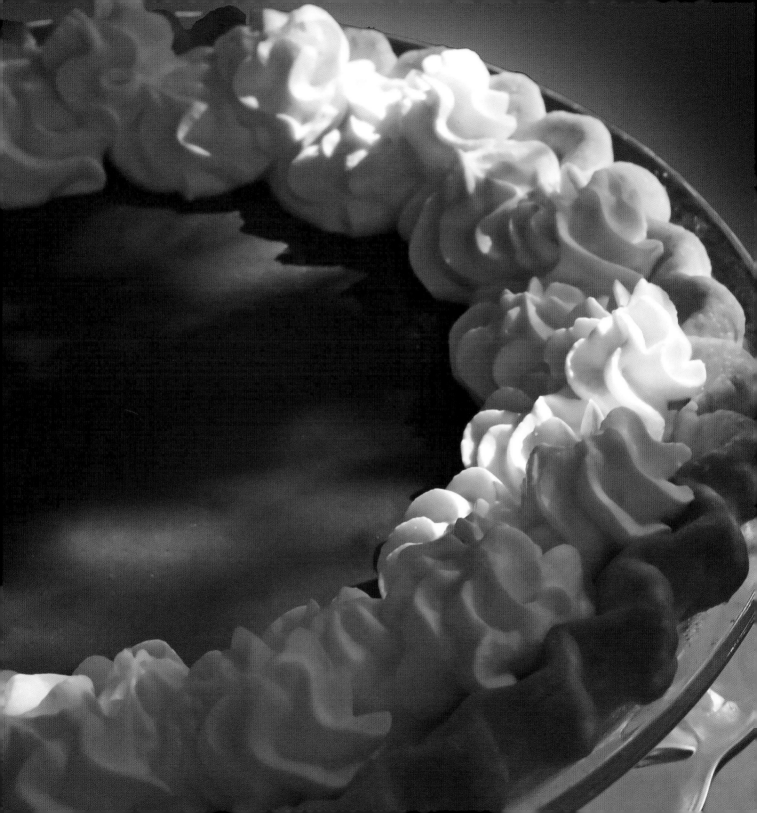

BEULAH LEDNER
DOBERGE CAKE

This creation originated with Beulah Ledner. She retired in 1949 and sold her recipes. The word Doberge is another one of those odd Orleanian words. The genesis is Dobos torte, which was created in Alasce-Lorraine. Once introduced to New Orleans, a few local improvements were made. To make a four, five, or six layer Doberge Cake from scratch is a labor-intensive project, but we learned a few shortcuts and tricks. Even easier is Duncan Hines® French Vanilla cake mix, which has a good flavor and texture.

YIELD: 9-INCH CAKE*

2 cups	cake flour, sifted	3 large	egg whites, beaten until stiff
1 teaspoon	baking soda	1 cup	buttermilk
10 tablespoons	unsalted butter	2 teaspoons	vanilla extract

Preheat oven to 300°F.

Line the bottom of the cake pans with baking parchment cut to fit two to four 9-inch round cake pans. In a medium bowl, sift the flour, soda, and salt 3 times. Cream the butter and sugar in a large mixing bowl, and add egg yolks, one at a time. Gradually alternate adding the flour mixture and buttermilk, then mix well by beating about 3 minutes. Fold in the 3 beaten egg whites, and vanilla. Bake for 45 minutes or until done. After the cake cools, split each layer in half to make 4 thin layers. Or simply use four or more cake pans and divide the batter evenly between them to avoid the mess of splitting them. Our record was 7 layers. Bake them two at a time, watching carefully. Since they are thin, they will cook quickly. A straw inserted into the layer comes out clean. Another test it to touch the top of the layer, and if it springs back nicely, it is done. Cool the cakes completely on wire racks then brush off the crumbs carefully.

CHOCOLATE FILLING

2-1/2 tablespoons	corn starch, sifted	2 cups	half-and-half
2/3 cup	granulated sugar	6 ounces	semi-sweet chocolate chips, melted
2 tablespoons	cocoa powder	1 ounce	unsweetened chocolate, melted
1/8 teaspoon	salt	1 tablespoon	unsalted butter, softened
1 cup	heavy whipping cream	2 teaspoons	vanilla extract
3 large	egg yolks, whisked		

In a medium heavy-bottomed saucepan, add the sifted cornstarch, sugar, cocoa powder, and salt. Slowly stir in the heavy whipping cream. Place pan over medium high heat, and temper the egg yolks by adding the well beaten egg yolks to the mixture very slowly while whipping very quickly. Tempering means do not add the eggs too quickly or the eggs will cook. Add the half-and-half, followed by the melted chocolate, stirring carefully but well. The chocolates will form little dark bits but will melt as mixture heats.

Bring mixture to a boil, stirring slowly but constantly using a wooden spoon. Do NOT use a whisk. (The vigorous whisking will apparently break down the starch molecules and lead to a runny mess). When it begins to boil, reduce heat to low, and slowly boil for 2 more minutes.

Press mixture through a fine sieve into a large bowl. Immediately add the butter and vanilla, stir well to incorporate, and place a piece of plastic wrap over surface to prevent a skin forming. Cool and refrigerate for 1-1/2 hours.

When the pudding has set up and is thick, spread evenly between each layer. Do NOT spread pudding on the top layer or on the sides of the cake-layer stack. We did. The following icing will slide off. It did.

The chocolate butter cream icing recipe is on page 90. Spread the icing on the top and sides of the assembled cake. Return to the refrigerator to harden before cutting.

It is not a real birthday in our family without a Doberge cake. We overnight it to various family members each year. Gambino's Bakery is always prepared to ship one frozen, posthaste.

Maurice's Pastries provide an especially delectable Doberge through Chef Jean Luc Albin. It must be ordered in advance. His bakery will festoon the cake with chocolate roses, leaves, names, special sentiments, or other decorations as requested.

One New Orleans innovation was preparing the cake in sheet pans then cutting it into 1-1/2 inch petit fours. If served as petit fours, however, expect to present all three flavors.

Traditionally Doberge is lemon, or chocolate. Indecisive consumers ask for the cake to be half lemon and half chocolate or caramel. The bakeries anticipate this and happily oblige.

There is a lemon filling recipe is on page 25, and any lemon butter cream icing recipe will top the cake.

For a double flavored Doberge cake, simply spread the different fillings halfway across the same side of each layer.

Leftovers are best consumed about midnight, while standing in front of an open refrigerator.

Carnival begins January 6, the feast of the Epiphany, and ends on Mardi Gras Day, French for Fat Tuesday, as the feast before the fast. Lent begins the next day on Ash Wednesday. The date for Mardi Gras day can be calculated by counting back 47 days before Easter.

King cake is a Mardi Gras custom and passion in New Orleans. Every carnival season our bakeries ship hundreds of thousands of the sweet ovals to ex-pats and other friends of the city.

Baked inside each King Cake is a tiny porcelain or plastic baby, representing the Christ child. The person who gets the baby must provide the next occasion's King Cake. Down here, we collect King Cake babies and we name them. The King Cake twins above are called Gabriel (TOP) and Ruben.

King Cake may be served as a coffee cake, or as dessert, sliced in 2- or 3- inch pieces. It may contain a variety of flavorings, or be nothing more than a plain yeast cake decorated with sugar glaze and colored sugar crystals. However, most of the recipes we tested for King Cake were complicated, messy, time-consuming, and a royal pain. This could be why we natives usually get ours at a bakery.

But should you wish to bake your own King Cake, be grateful that Susan Hennessey, a long-time assistant and treasured friend, found a simple, store-bought solution.

SUSAN HENNESSEY

KING CAKE

Bright sugar crystals represent the Mardi Gras colors of purple for justice, green for faith, and gold for power. Skip the tedious cake making process by using Pillsbury® Hot Roll mix instead. Prepare it according to the package directions but roll it out, fill, shape, and ice it according to the following King Cake directions.

YIELD: SERVES 12

KING CAKE

1 box	Pillsbury® Hot Roll Mix, 16 ounces
1/2 cup	granulated sugar for filling
1-1/2 teaspoons	cinnamon for filling
1/3 cup	unsalted butter, room temperature

Preheat oven to 375°F.

Cream the butter, sugar, and cinnamon together until soft enough to spread easily.

Follow directions on the Pillsbury® Hot Roll Mix package. Turn one half of the dough onto a floured surface, and roll into a 2- foot x 1- foot rectangle. Spread half of the butter and filling mixture on top of the dough.

Taking a good thing a step farther, many bakeries now stuff their King Cakes with ingredients such as apple, peach, or cherry pie filling, cream cheese, or chopped pecans with cinnamon sugar. Use your creative imagination.

Beginning at the wide edge, roll the dough toward you into a long cigar shape approximately 2 inches in diameter. Do the same with the second half of the dough. Place dough roll seam side down on a well greased baking sheet, and curve each roll, pinching the ends together to make oval ring. Cover, and let rise in warm place for 20 minutes or until doubled in size. Bake at 375°F for 15 to 20 minutes or until a straw inserted into the dough comes out clean. Allow the cake to cool.

GLAZE

2 cups	confectioners' sugar, sifted
2 tablespoons	lemon juice
2 tablespoons	water

COLORED SUGAR CRYSTALS

1 cup	granulated sugar, large crystals
3 or 4 drops	green food coloring
3 or 4 drops	purple food coloring
3 or 4 drops	yellow food coloring

To prepare the glaze, combine sugar, lemon juice, and water mixing until smooth. Slowly add more water by the teaspoon until it spreads as easily as a thin icing.

Place 1/3 cup sugar in each of three small jars with lids. Add three drops of food coloring in each one. Cover with lid, and shake until color is evenly distributed throughout the large sugar crystals. Add food coloring, drop by drop until the desired shade is achieved.

Coat the top of the oval king cake with glaze. Immediately sprinkle the colored sugars in 2- to- 3 inch alternating rows of purple, green and gold. Cut and serve.

LA CUISINE
LEMON ICEBOX PIE

Lemon icebox pie is beautiful to behold and to present. Many families have a personal recipe passed down from generation to generation. Others insist that Mr. Ed, from the now extinct La Cuisine on Harrison Avenue near the Lakefront, had the ultimate version. This is the restaurant's recipe.

YIELD: 8-INCH PIE

CRUST:

44	vanilla wafers
	(one box makes 2 crusts)
1/4 cup	granulated sugar
1/2 cup	unsalted butter, melted

FILLING:

2 cans	sweetened condensed milk
4 large	egg yolks
3/4 cup	fresh lemon juice,
6	medium lemons
2 rounded tablespoons	lemon zest (very fine)
1 or 2 drops	yellow food coloring

Preheat oven to 375°F.

Crush vanilla wafers in a food processor or use a rolling pin. Add the sugar, and melted butter, and blend well. Press into bottom, and along sides of a Pyrex pie baking dish. Bake at 375°F for approximately 8 minutes or until the crust is lightly browned.

Reset the oven to 350°F.

Combine sweetened condensed milk with egg yolks, and blend well. Slowly pour in lemon juice stirring constantly. Add a tablespoon of lemon zest and taste for sufficient lemon juice. Add one or two drops of yellow food coloring and mix well. Sprinkle the remaining lemon zest on the bottom of the pie crust. Pour lemon mixture into the pie crust.

MERINGUE:

7 large	egg whites, room temperature
1/2 cup	granulated sugar
1/8 teaspoon	cream of tartar

In a perfectly clean bowl, using a handheld electric mixer, beat the egg whites. When the whites start to become foamy, and soft peaks begin to form, slowly add the sugar, and then the cream of tartar. Beat until fairly stiff peaks form, and the whites are glossy. Mound on top of filling, and create decorative swirls. Spread meringue to overlap edges of pie crust slightly (meringue shrinks during baking). Bake in 350°F oven until slightly brown, approximately 12 to 15 minutes.

Refrigerate until set, approximately 1-1/2 hours.

Lemon icebox pie is a Southern tradition, but there is little agreement on specific recipes. Clancey's uptown serves a splendid version, close in sweet, creamy tartness to La Cuisine's stellar pie.

Former Orleanian, and Louisiana native, Sue Anna Cellini treasures a secret family recipe. It has caused her and Dando, her husband, both attorneys, to be courted for their dinner invitations across the country.

Michele Vine persuasively argues that her mother properly used a square Pyrex dish for her crust recipe. She would completely cover the bottom with whole vanilla wafers, then ring the sides of the dish with wafers standing on end. No further effort was necessary, she simply poured the lemon mixture over the wafers, and topped the dish with meringue.

Some cooks prefer a different crust. It is also impossible to decide the merits of vanilla wafers versus graham cracker crusts. Personal opinion prevails. You decide. It is a judgment call.

A friend and I were helping a pal get ready for her son's wedding. In honor of the bride and groom's heritages, family members had been asked to bring a special dessert to the rehearsal dinner.

Some relatives were Italian, others Greek. Then there were a couple of Texans, some New Yorkers and a few Orleanians. It would be an international buffet of sweets.

What a lovely idea.

We would help the mother-of-the-groom stay calm by baking with her, we assured ourselves. Hours later, many sticky hours, 200 individual bite-sized pies representing New Orleans and Texas were beautifully arranged. As it turned out, far too many, but the extras went home with the guests. What had we been thinking?

Now, whenever we feel an excess of enthusiasm overtaking us, the words "pecan pie" are guaranteed to slow us down for more reflection.

CAMELLIA GRILL
PECAN PIE

At the river's bend where St. Charles Avenue winds into Carrolton Avenue, Camellia Grill has enough colorful history as an old-fashioned diner with a matching menu to attract both locals and visitors. Pecan pie is alleged to be a magical cure for most anything after a night out, and would soothe any sweet tooth. Following a hiatus, during which patrons left love notes on the locked door, Camellia Grill has returned.

In the old days, eagerly waiting patrons were served by gregarious waiters with flair, flourish, and linen napkins. A counter stool was an absolutely democratic experience based on the place in line. Parties were ruthlessly divided, and sent to any empty stool. Otherwise, a group could wait to sit together once the spaces were available. On the way out, any request for the pecan pie recipe was happily fulfilled.

YIELD: 9-INCH PIE

4 large	eggs		1-1/4 cups	brown sugar, firmly packed
1/4 teaspoon	salt		1 teaspoon	vanilla extract
1/4 cup	unsalted butter, melted		9-inch	pie shell (unbaked)
1-1/4 cups	light corn syrup		1 cup	pecans, chopped or whole

Preheat oven to 350°F.

Make a pie shell according to the recipe on page 83, or use a prepared unbaked pie crust.

In a medium sized bowl beat eggs with a wire whisk or fork until foamy. Add the salt, melted butter, light corn syrup, brown sugar, and vanilla extract. Mix well. Pour into unbaked pastry shell; top the mixture with chopped or whole pecans.

Bake at 350°F for approximately 45 to 50 minutes.

Remove from oven, and cool on a wire rack to room temperature before cutting. Serve topped with a scoop of vanilla ice cream for pie â la mode, or add a swirl of whipped cream.

CHEF WARREN LERUTH
PAVE AU CHOCOLATE

Densely chocolate, Chef Warren LeRuth's Pavé au Chocolate is a forerunner to the now famous flourless chocolate cake. Both Commander's Palace and Arnaud's, among many other restaurants, have their own versions, and chocolate lovers rejoice. Chef LeRuth delighted in keeping secret a few ingredients from the recipes he generously handed out, with only minor sins of omission. He always wanted the dishes he prepared to taste just a little better than the one you made at home. Sadly, he never published a major cookbook, only two small pamphlets, one to celebrate his restaurant's 20th anniversary, and the other named *Front Door, Back Door*. This recipe is from the former, and is accurate, with nothing omitted.

YIELD: 8 SERVINGS

8-inch	cake pan	12 ounces	unsalted butter, melted
12 ounces	dark chocolate	1 tablespoon	LeRuth's Vanilla Bean
12 large	eggs, separated		Marinade

Melt the chocolate in a double boiler. Beat the egg yolks, and slowly fold into the chocolate. Then, fold in the melted butter and vanilla bean marinade. In a separate bowl, whip egg whites until they are stiff, and fold carefully into the chocolate mixture. Line the bottom of the cake pan with a circle of baking parchment cut to fit. Pour the mixture into the cake pan and cover.

Chill overnight.

Garnish with your imagination.

The fleur de lis cookie at the right is a New Orleans' symbol. The recipe for it is located on page 59. The template may be created in any shape desired.

To serve, slice into small pie-shaped wedges. Top with whipped cream or place a slice in a puddle of crème anglaise (recipe on page 91). Garnish with fruit coulis or fresh fruit.

YIELD: 1 CUP

FRUIT COULIS

1 cup	fresh fruit (berries are preferred)	3 tablespoons	orange juice
		1 tablespoon	lemon juice
1/4 cup	water or fruit juice	2 tablespoons	granulated sugar

Cook in water to cover over medium heat until soft, approximately 5 minutes, and drain. Add juice or water, add orange juice, and lemon juice. Heat until warm. Press through a fine sieve or use a blender to puree. While mixture is still hot, stir in the sugar until it is dissolved.

New Orleans as a city for fine dining beyond Creole cuisine came to national attention in 1965 when the late Chef Warren LeRuth renovated a Victorian shotgun cottage across the Mississippi River in old Gretna. He stirred our culinary world forever.

Irascible, and exacting, Warren was not only creative but also a fearlessly innovative chef. In food circles he was the Renaissance man who did things his own way. Rather than expand with his restaurant's popularity, he removed tables.

Generous with his time and talent he developed dishes for other restaurateurs, and many of those recipes remain as standards of their kind. Fond memories from the chefs he mentored, former guests, and friends keep his memory as vibrant as his food.

As a research chef, Warren developed many products including a special vanilla bean marinade, which is still the crème de la crème of flavorings. LeRuth's Vanilla Bean Marinade is liquid gold. It is available from several web sites.

Strawberry Shortcake

Food critic and restaurant gadfly Tom Fitzmorris' book *New Orleans Food* was published to great success and well deserved applause. He offered us his most delectable recipe for strawberry shortcakes, but I could not leave well enough alone. The addition of blueberries makes perfect sense especially on the 4th of July. Raspberries or any fresh seasonal fruit would be delicious. Otherwise, the recipe is vintage Tom: squishy and sweet inside, surprisingly tart with a crunchy exterior.

Louisiana produces brilliant strawberries–bright red, plump, and sweet. When an early freeze is threatened, it is breaking news locally as farmers rush to protect their tender crops, and aficionados fret until the danger passes.

In New Orleans we prefer our shortcake served as biscuits rather than as a whole cake, however, you may use cake cut into serving slices. There are no rules. An angel food cake, meringue shells, yellow layer cake, or the small cake shells all work equally well. You choose.

YIELD: 12 SHORTCAKES

4 cups	self-rising flour	1- 3/4 cup	fresh strawberries
3/4 cup	granulated sugar		or other berries
1 stick	butter	2 pints	half-and-half or whipping cream

Preheat oven to 475°F.

Combine the flour, and sugar into a large bowl. Whisk to blend. Cut butter into flour mixture, and stir in with a wire whisk until mixture resembles coarse cornmeal. A few small lumps are fine.

Blend in the half-and-half with light strokes of a kitchen fork. Continue lightly blending until the dough leaves the side of the bowl. Add a little more milk if necessary to work all the dry ingredients into a sticky, thoroughly damp dough.

Spoon out the dough with a tablespoon, and drop biscuits about four inches in diameter, and two inches high on a greased cookie sheet. Bake 10 to 14 minutes. Use the middle or top rack in the oven. The biscuits are ready when they are lightly brown on the top. Dark brown indicates over baking.

Wash and remove the stem leaves from the strawberries. Slice them top to bottom about 1/4 inch thick. Sprinkle with sugar, and marinate covered overnight in the refrigerator.

WHIPPED CREAM

1 pint	heavy whipping cream
1/3 cup	granulated sugar

Whip the heavy whipping cream in a chilled metal bowl until soft peaks form. Add the sugar, and continue whipping until no grittiness remains.

Slice the shortcakes in half. Drizzle the secret marinade over each half. Spoon some whipped cream on the bottom half. Add sliced strawberries until they fall off the sides, and a little more whipped cream.

Mother was a World War II bride who simply could not imagine why anyone would not take full advantage of the new convenience foods out of cans and from boxes that had been developed during the war. The truth is that she could not cook. With one glorious exception – strawberry shortcake.

Her strawberry shortcake was dazzling. She was a wizard. On special occasions the seven of us headed for the French Market for flats of strawberries. We would wash, hull, and slice them. Then mother made her magic.

The strawberries were sprinkled with sugar, then covered, and refrigerated overnight. The next day she would drain the remaining liquid and mash a strawberry or two into it. Today, I'd add a tablespoon of Chambord®. Before assembling, and serving, she'd drizzle this secret marinade over the split shortcakes.

She got the biscuit recipe from the side of a Bisquick® box, and the whipped cream from a pressurized can.

As the oldest child, early on, I cherished the Girl Scout Cookbook. My three sisters became excellent cooks to save themselves from egg salad and blueberry pancakes. Mother's first grandson was also fed her boxed and canned specialties at family gatherings. He was sufficiently driven to become a chef. Hunger is an instinctual motivation.

CHEF LEAH CHASE
Sweet Potato Pie

There's something about a sweet potato pie that feels like home when it's presented. No one has a bigger heart than Leah Chase. She'll give you a hug as warm as her smile, and a great meal. Loved ones and guests receive her enthusiastic generosity for beautiful food, and Leah enjoys seeing appreciative diners in return. Not only is her sweet potato filling as succulent as it promises, but her pecan crust is also unique.

YIELD: 8-INCH PIE, SERVES 6

PIE FILLING:

4 large	sweet potatoes, boiled until tender and peeled		1 teaspoon	ground cinnamon
			1/2 cup	sweetened condensed milk
1 cup	granulated sugar		1/4 cup	unsalted butter, melted

In a large bowl, mash the sweet potatoes. Add in the sugar and cinnamon, and mix well. Add condensed milk and melted butter. Whisk mixture until smooth and bright orange. Set aside.

CRUST:

1 cup	all-purpose flour		5 tablespoons	vegetable shortening
1 teaspoon	salt		1/2 cup	water, cold
1/4 cup	pecans, finely chopped		sprinkle	cinnamon

Preheat oven to 450°F.

In a medium sized bowl stir flour and salt together, and add pecans. Cut in shortening until it is in small, pea-sized lumps. Slowly add the water, and mix into stiff paste.

On a floured board, roll out the dough into a 10-inch circle, and place into 8-inch pie pan. Prick the bottom with a fork several times.

Bake for a few minutes, until the crust is barely cooked. Remove from the oven, and lower the temperature to 350°F.

Fill pie shell with sweet potato mixture. Sprinkle top lightly with cinnamon. Return the pie to the oven, and bake for 35 minutes, until set.

Cool to room temperature or chill, and serve.

Chef Leah Chase has been cooking for more than fifty years. She and her husband Dooky, Jr. transformed a tiny sandwich shop into a celebrated restaurant.

Dooky Chase's quickly became a political hub and haven during the Civil Rights Movement, and no one ever left hungry; Leah made certain of that, and still does.

Her smile and gracious manner let you know immediately that she's a lady—a lady to be reckoned with. Her charitable, civic and professional efforts have been repeatedly recognized, although she seeks nothing but to feed her guests properly and serve her community.

She was one of the seventy-five women featured in "I Dream A World: Portraits of Black Women Who Changed America," she received the National Candace Award as one of the ten most outstanding black women in the country, was the recipient of the New Orleans Times-Picayune's Loving Cup, and was given the Ella Brennan Savoir Faire Award for Excellence by the National Federation of Chefs. The James Beard Society has also honored her. She's authored two cookbooks and an autobiography.

Leah has received awards from the Anti-Defamation League, and the NAACP, as well as honorary doctorate degrees from Holy Cross College in New Orleans and Madonna College in Detroit.

CUSTARDS & PUDDINGS

Custards and puddings are the chef's balancing act of taste, texture, temperature and are the razzmatazz of New Orleans' desserts. Creamy custards and puddings may be simple or complex, may soothe or surprise.

Summer Cream was my dessert specialty as a young woman living in the Vieux Carré. It could be created quickly with fresh fruit from the nearby French Market. The recipe was a snap and met my criteria. Quick. Inexpensive. Delicious. Mix two or three tablespoons of brown sugar with a carton of sour cream then toss it gently with any colorful fruits or berries that were in season.

My place was as miniscule as my budget. It had been renovated into apartments many decades earlier and originally had been the historic Spanish stables on rue Governor Nicholls.

During the early 1800s, ladies and gentlemen sent their horses and carriages to the stables, much like commercial garages today. Gaming rooms on the second level above the stalls were for the drivers' amusement, while they awaited a return trip.

The property is still residential. The tenants, past and present, notable and notorious, as well are still particularly entertaining in the finest tradition of the stables.

Christopher Blake, a renowned former restaurateur and author, also lived there but in an exquisitely grand apartment. He demonstrated the way to easy elegance with his Summer Cream recipe. "Treat the best available, fresh and lovely ingredients with respect," he counseled me.

Words to remember.

BREAD PUDDING

Fans of casual Cajun cooking are much more concerned with food than fanfare. The Bon Ton's bread pudding is a bodacious standard, studded with raisins, and draped in a creamy whiskey sauce, served in a bustling restaurant. Aficionados insist that this is the city's best, quintessential, and definitive bread pudding. Others use the same words to tout bread pudding from other restaurants, and there is a long-standing and heart-felt argument over whether raisins should be used at all. What's the answer? Do what you like. It's simply a matter of personal good taste.

YIELD: 12 SERVINGS

5 cups	French bread cut in 1-inch cubes	2 cups	granulated sugar
1 quart	whole milk	2 tablespoons	vanilla extract
3 large	eggs	1 teaspoon	ground cinnamon
		1 cup	raisins (optional)
		3 tablespoons	unsalted butter, melted

Preheat oven to 350°F.

Tear the bread into 1-inch pieces, and soak them in the milk. Squeeze gently to make certain that the milk has soaked through. Add eggs, sugar, vanilla, cinnamon, raisins, and stir well.*

Pour melted butter into the bottom of a heavy 9- x 14- inch baking pan or into individual soufflé cups. Add the bread mixture. Sprinkle more cinnamon, and raisins on top if desired. Our test cooks preferred to place the soufflé cups into a large pan, filled with an inch of water. Place in a preheated oven, and bake 40 to 50 minutes or until a knife inserted about 2 inches from the center comes out clean. Do not overcook.

While the bread pudding is baking, prepare the whiskey sauce.

WHISKEY SAUCE

1 cup	granulated sugar
1 stick	butter, softened (4 ounces)
1 large	egg, beaten
1/4 cup	bourbon, rum, or cognac

Cool the bread pudding to room temperature. Cut baked bread pudding into 3-inch squares, and place on individual dessert dishes or serve in soufflé cups. Top with warmed whiskey sauce when ready to serve.

In a small bowl, cream the sugar, and butter together. Cook in a double boiler until very hot, and the sugar is well-dissolved. Temper the egg by gradually whisking the butter and sugar mixture into the egg. Tempering means do not add the hot butter too quickly or the eggs will scramble. Allow the sauce to cool, and stir in liquor of choice. Stir whiskey sauce before serving.

To warm the whiskey sauce, heat under broiler for 1 to 2 minutes, watching carefully.

Around lunch time on any business day the revolving doors of New Orleans' major office buildings spin and eject a steady stream of lawyers, bankers, and executives. They carry their appetites instead of briefcases to the nearby Bon Ton Café.

The serving staff and bartenders are experienced. When regular customers enter the unpretentious dining room, drinks can be placed on their regular tables as they are seated.

The Bon Ton is a classic, casual old New Orleans restaurant with checkered tablecloths and white uniforms. The difference at dinner is the table candles are lit.

Long owned by the Pierce family, the Bon Ton serves authentic, more traditional Cajun cuisine from century old family recipes, like this one handed down long ago from Alzina Pierce, since updated by proprietor Wayne Pierce.

Pierce maintains the family customs of fine food and warm hospitality from this lovely old brick building embellished with original cast-iron architectural features.

BREAD PUDDING SOUFFLÉ

Bread Pudding has been elevated to new heights by Commander's Bread Pudding Soufflé. Don't let the word *soufflé* deter you. This special dessert is a culinary sleight of hand created by combining prepared bread pudding with meringue, then baking it. Since the meringue provides the light, fluffy texture, there is no puff of air to fall. The bread pudding is baked in an 8-inch square pan. The meringue is made and incorporated into the baked bread pudding. The bread pudding-meringue mixture is then is then divided equally into six ramekins for the next step of baking and serving.

YIELD: 6 SERVINGS

BREAD PUDDING

3/4 cup	granulated sugar
1 teaspoon	ground cinnamon
pinch	nutmeg
3 large	eggs
1/3 cup	raisins (optional)

1 cup	heavy whipping cream
1 teaspoon	vanilla extract
5 cups	French bread cut in 1-inch cubes
butter	to grease baking pan or ramekin cups

MERINGUE

9 large	egg whites, room temperature
3/4 cups	granulated sugar
1/4 teaspoon	cream of tartar

WHISKEY SAUCE

1 cup	heavy whipping cream
1/2 tablespoon	cornstarch
1 tablespoon	water, room temperature
3 tablespoons	granulated sugar
1/4 cup	bourbon (2 ounces)

Preheat the oven to 350°F.

Grease an 8-inch square baking pan. In a large bowl, combine and mix the sugar, cinnamon, and nutmeg. Whisk in the eggs until smooth, then whisk in the heavy whipping cream, and the vanilla extract. Add the bread cubes, tossing to coat evenly, then let stand about 10 minutes to allow the bread to soak up the custard.

Place the raisins in a greased pan and top with the egg mixture. Bake 25 to 30 minutes, or until the pudding has a golden brown color, and is firm to the touch. Insert a toothpick in the center. If it comes out clean, it is done. The pudding should be moist. Cool to room temperature.

Meringue: This dish needs a good, stiff meringue. In a large mixing clean bowl whip egg whites with the cream of tartar until foamy. Add the sugar gradually. Continue whipping until shiny, and firm peaks form.

In a large bowl break half the bread pudding into pieces using your hands or a spoon. Gently fold in 1/4 of the meringue. Add a portion of this base to each of the ramekins. Place the remaining bread pudding in the bowl, break into pieces, and carefully fold in the rest of the meringue. Top the ramekins to about 1-1/2 inches above the rim with this lighter mixture. Smooth, and shape tops with spoon into a dome over the ramekin rim. Bake immediately for approximately 20 minutes or until golden brown. Make the whiskey sauce while the bread pudding soufflés are baking.

To prepare the whiskey sauce, place the cream in a small saucepan over medium heat, and bring to a boil. Whisk corn starch, and water together, then add to the heavy whipping cream while whisking. Bring to a boil. Whisk and let simmer for a few seconds, taking care not to burn the mixture on the bottom. Remove from heat. Stir in the sugar, and the bourbon. Cool to room temperature. Serve immediately. At the table, poke a hole in the top of each soufflé, and pour the room temperature whiskey sauce inside.

New Orleans' most gracious culinary matriarch, Ella Brennan, first made her mark on the Brennan's of Royal Street establishment, prior to the rambling family's division of restaurants.

Ella, her sister Dottie, and her brother Dick revitalized Commander's Palace. They introduced their children to the business, spawning even more restaurants. Ti Adelaide Martin and Lally Brennan are this generation's co-proprietors. They have beautifully renovated and invigorated Commander's from top to bottom, kitchens to dining rooms.

Probably the most respected legend in the restaurant world, Ella set high standards that are followed today. Paul Prudhomme, Emeril Lagasse, and the late Jamie Shannon were executive chefs under her reign.

Laughing with us following brunch one Sunday, Chef Jamie took us into Commander's pastry kitchen for a demonstration of how to make Bread Pudding Soufflé. He was magically talented. Jamie left far too soon, and left a hole in our hearts, but he also left behind his contributions to a grand legacy.

In the Garden District, surrounded by oak trees, and sprawling onto a leafy courtyard, the restaurant continues to flourish.

Bread Pudding is one of those happy desserts that lends itself to many variations on the same theme, as long as the main components remain.

The Palace Café's version features white chocolate with tongue-in-cheek brown chocolate sprinkles.

White chocolate is an ivory confection made from cocoa butter without the cocoa solids. It also includes flavorings such as vanilla. It is not considered chocolate, since it does not include cocoa, but it tastes similar to milk chocolate.

WHITE CHOCOLATE SAUCE

8 ounces	white chocolate
3 ounces	heavy whipping cream
1 ounce	semi-sweet chocolate

In the top of a double boiler over hot water, melt the white chocolate. Remove from heat, and mix in heavy whipping cream.

After ladling the sauce over the bread pudding, garnish with chocolate curls or crumbles.

PALACE CAFÉ
WHITE CHOCOLATE BREAD PUDDING

Owned and operated by Dickie Brennan of the sprawling restaurant family, the upbeat Palace Café is located in the historic Werlein building on Canal Street, where musicians used to get their sheet music, and instruments. Today, Bitsy Werlein continues the music business in Metairie, a suburb, while Dickie serves New Orleans' food that is music to your mouth. The Palace Café's most popular dessert is white chocolate bread pudding, a creative riff on the classic with quite a different flavor.

YIELD: 8 SERVINGS

5 cups	French bread, sliced into 1/4 inch pieces		10 ounces	white chocolate
3 tablespoons	butter or margarine, melted		1 cup	whole milk
			1/2 cup	granulated sugar
3 cups	whipping cream		8 large	eggs yolks
			2 large	eggs

Preheat oven to 275°F.

Bake the French bread in the oven 15 minutes to dry it. Remove from oven, and set aside.

Pour butter into a 9- x 13- inch baking pan. Heat the 3 cups of whipping cream in a double boiler, and add 10 ounces of crumbled white chocolate. When the chocolate is melted, remove from the heat.

In another double boiler, heat the milk, sugar, eggs, and egg yolks until warm. Gradually add the egg mixture stirring quickly as it is poured, into the cream, and chocolate mixture.

Place the bread pieces into a greased baking pan. Pour 1/2 of the mixture over the bread, and let settle until the bread soaks up all the liquid. Pour the remaining mixture over the top. Cover with aluminum foil, and bake 1 hour. Prepare the white chocolate sauce while the bread pudding is baking.

Remove the foil from the bread pudding after 1 hour, and bake approximately 15 minutes more until the top is golden brown. Cool to room temperature. To serve, cut into 3 inch squares, and place on individual serving dishes.

Warm the white chocolate sauce. Spoon over baked, warm bread pudding, and garnish with white chocolate curls or brown chocolate crumbles. To make chocolate crumbles rub a piece of hard chocolate over a small cheese grater. To make the chocolate curls, soften the chocolate slightly and use a potato peeler to run down the edge of the bar.

ARNAUD'S
CRÉME BRÛLÉE

When Archie and Jane Casbarian acquired Arnaud's, a legendary New Orleans establishment, in 1978 they added Crème Brûlée to their first menu. It is a treasured family recipe passed down from Jane's honorary aunt, Joan Rosenberg, who had introduced Archie and Jane. It was one of the first appearances of Crème Brûlée in an American restaurant, and definitely the first in New Orleans. The dessert has now swept the country, and can be tricked out by adding fruit and other flavorful ingredients. At Arnaud's, Crème Brûlée is served classically just as it was designed. The French translation is literally "burned cream."

YIELD: 6 SERVINGS

6 large	egg yolks	1 tablespoon	vanilla extract
1/3 cup	granulated sugar	3 tablespoons	dark brown sugar
2-1/2 cups	heavy whipping cream		

Preheat the oven to 250°F.

In a medium bowl with the mixer set at medium speed, beat the egg yolks and sugar together and set aside. In a saucepan over medium heat, bring the cream to a boil. Remove from heat immediately. Add to the egg and sugar mixture, continuing to beat. Add the vanilla extract and continue to beat until the mixture is completely cooled.

Pour the cooled mixture into six 4-ounce custard cups. Line the sides of a 3 inch high baking pan with parchment paper, then place the cups in the pan. Add hot water until it reaches halfway up the sides of the cups. (The paper stabilizes the water and prevents the cups from shaking.)

Bake for 50 minutes. Remove the cups from the pan. Cool to room temperature, and refrigerate until chilled.

Sprinkle 1/2 tablespoon of the brown sugar over the top of each cup. Place the cups on a baking sheet, and set under a hot broiler until the sugar melts, darkens, and forms a crust. This is the brûlée process, so watch it carefully. A nifty little butane torch is available in many gourmet shops, and may also be used to caramelize the sugar topping. As the sugar crust cools, it hardens. Refrigerate until ready to serve.

The best part of the dessert is cracking the top layer sharply with a spoon to discover the creamy goodness underneath.

Arnaud's in the historic French Quarter is a leader of the culinary old guard, encompassing 13 historic buildings.

During the mid-1800s, restaurants in New Orleans graduated from serving rough workmen to establishments more suitable for ladies and gentlemen. In 1918, a French wine salesman, Arnaud Cazenave, founded the grand restaurant that still bears his name. It opened just as the heyday of dining out exploded and is one of the few originals that thrives to this day.

Archie and Jane Casbarian acquired the venerable establishment, continuing the tradition of family ownership. They immediately began an extensive restoration, and with the renaissance of Arnaud's, the city celebrated a legend's return to grandeur.

"Tonight," wrote Archie in his inaugural menu on February 28, 1979, "marks the rebirth of a grand, and noble restaurant. We herald a new era in the long history of a world-famous establishment."

Flickering lanterns lead down rue Bienville to sparkling beveled glass windows that overlook a historic dining room of chandeliers, ceiling fans, and mosaic floors.

A prominent restaurant family, their son Archie, and their daughter Katy, the next generation, are now active in Arnaud's management.

Since 1905

Galatoire's is another time-honored Creole restaurant maintained by a multi-generational family of proprietors. Located on bawdy Bourbon Street, it's an oasis of civilization for high society and sometimes low behavior that can cause a flurry of controversy or become something to ignore in polite company.

Galatoire's is as much a New Orleans experience as it is a culinary excursion.

The restaurant is a local's favorite. Friday lunches are an opportunity to gather, gossip, show off a new outfit, and indulge in delicious excess. The well-placed mirrors allow guests to surreptitiously inspect each other, with whom they are dining, a coiffure, or one's demeanor.

Dressed in classic ceiling fans, mosaic tile floors, and mirrored walls, Galatoire's has been serving Orleanians for more than a century.

There time stands still, generations of patrons order the same dishes as their forefathers, and tradition is underscored.

Founded in 1905 by Jean Galatoire, the revered establishment received the 2005 James Beard San Pellegrino Outstanding Restaurant award.

Galatoire's Restaurant is overseen by Chief Operating Officer Melvin Rodrigue. He works in close conjunction with David Gooch (grandson of Leon), Justin Frey (grandson of Justin) and Michele Galatoire (granddaughter of Leon), and Executive Chef Brian Landry.

GALATOIRE'S
CRÈME CARAMEL

Galatoire's crème caramel, or cup custard as we call it, is one of New Orleans' most traditional, beloved desserts. Orleanians believe in comfort food and crème caramel comes pretty close as a benchmark. Mild, silky, and barely sweet, it can be a child's first grown-up dessert in a restaurant, or an adult's culinary hug. It slips from spoon to tongue without stopping in between except for one barely discernible, succulent moment that you may never forget.

YIELD: 12 CUP CUSTARDS

2-1/2 cups	granulated sugar
1/2 cup	water, room temperature
1 quart	whole milk
10 large	eggs
2 tablespoons	vanilla extract

Preheat oven to 350°F.

CARAMEL SAUCE

Melt 1 cup of the sugar in a small heavy saucepan over a medium heat, swirling occasionally, for 8 to 10 minutes. When the sugar turns golden brown, add 1/2 cup of water, and using a long-handled spoon slowly stir in the water. Cook the caramel sauce for 2 to 3 minutes, stirring constantly. Remove the pan from the heat. Into each of 12 custard cups or ramekins, pour enough hot caramel to coat the bottom. Put the custard cups in a 2-inch deep baking pan, and fill the pan with very hot water until it comes halfway up the sides of the cups. Set the cups aside while making the custard.

CUSTARD

Heat the milk in a large pan over medium high heat until it simmers, watching carefully. Remove from the heat. In a separate bowl combine the remaining 1-1/2 cups of sugar, the eggs, and the vanilla extract. Whisk until smooth. Slowly add the milk to the eggs to temper them and avoid scrambling the eggs. Once all of the milk has been incorporated, pour the custard mix through a fine-mesh strainer.

Fill each of the caramel coated cups with the liquid custard. Cover the pan with foil, and create a seal at the edges. Bake the custards in the water bath for 30 minutes.

Remove the foil, and bake for an additional 30 to 40 minutes. To check for doneness, touch the top of custard. It should have a light, springy texture that does not stick to your finger.

Remove the custards from the water bath, let them cool to room temperature, and refrigerate until chilled.

Separate the custards from the sides of the cups using a small paring knife. Invert the cups onto small desert plates or bowls. Remove the cups to allow the rich caramel sauce to run down the sides of the custards.

CHEF GERARD CROZIER
FLOATING ISLAND

Floating Island seemed to be a thing of our past, until we rediscovered it at Crozier's, another New Orleans restaurant memory that lingers on many taste buds. Chef Gerard Crozier, a native of Lyon, brought Eveline, his wife, his culinary sensibilities, and a Floating Island recipe from France. Friday evenings at Crozier's were especially delightful and the only time just a few servings of his silky Floating Island were available. Connoisseurs of the dessert were careful to keep this treat to themselves, often calling ahead to reserve their portions.

YIELD: FOUR 1/2 CUP SERVINGS

4 large	eggs, separated	garnish	(optional)
1 cup	granulated sugar, plus	1 cup	seasonal berries
3/4 cup	for sauce	4	fresh mint sprigs
2 cups	whole milk		
1/2	vanilla bean, halved length-wise, reserve seeds		
1/2 cup	water, room temperature		

In a perfectly clean bowl, beat room temperature egg whites with an electric mixer slowly at first. Gradually add 1/4 cup of sugar then continue to beat at high speed until very stiff peaks form.

Split the vanilla bean lengthwise and scrape the seeds from the pod.

In a heavy saucepan over a medium heat, scald the milk, adding 1/4 cup of sugar and the vanilla beans. Stir until the sugar has dissolved.

Drop large tablespoon-sized dollops of the beaten egg white, and sugar mixture onto the surface of the milk. Poach the egg whites for 4 to 5 minutes, turning once, creating the islands. Remove them from the milk carefully with a slotted spoon, and set aside on a platter. Reserve the remaining milk.

Beat the egg yolks in a medium bowl with 1/2 cup of sugar and add the hot milk, stirring vigorously. Cool and strain through a fine mesh sieve. Set aside.

Make a caramel sauce by boiling the remaining 3/4 cup of sugar and 1/2 cup of water for approximately 5 minutes until it reaches a syrup consistency.

When ready to serve, pour equal amounts of the remaining milk mixture into 4 shallow bowls. Using a slotted spoon, carefully slip the islands to float atop each serving. If desired, drizzle warm caramel sauce in swirls across top. Add seasonal berries, and fresh mint as a garnish if desired.

Variation: Rather than a caramel drizzle, puree fresh seasonal berries to create a coulis, and drizzle with that color instead. The recipe for fruit coulis is on page 29.

Floating Island is reminiscent of certain times when temperature and atmospheric conditions are in alignment and a fog layer drifts on the surface of the Mississippi River. Above the great puffs and curls, clear sky and the riverbank's crescent reveal themselves in vivid colors. Dockside, a paddle wheeler with calliope singing waits to churn into the river.

It's an old-fashioned dessert, a serving of pure bliss. It came to Louisiana via France, traveling the same route across the ocean as did so many of our great recipes.

My husband's family cook was Anna Bolan, who joined them shortly before Billy was born. She possessed an astonishing memory. Once a recipe was discussed, no matter how complex, she would prepare it flawlessly.

She would add her refinements, always improving and making the recipe her own.

Before she retired, Anna allowed me to spend many hours assisting—more watching rather than being of any real help—as she cooked. Floating Island was a family favorite and prepared whenever Anna felt that the occasion required a festive dessert.

Chef Besh presides over Restaurant August's menu and kitchen with style and the grace of classical training.

Chocolate usually flavors Pot du Crème, however Chef Besh created a playful café-au-lait-taste twist with the good humor of beignets as a side sweet.

Considered one of New Orleans stellar young chefs, he breaks new ground and continues to enhance the city's culinary reputation. He has been honored with the James Beard Award, and Restaurant August has been named one of the top 50 restaurants in the country.

CHEF JOHN BESH

POT DU CRÈME CAFÉ AU LAIT WITH BEIGNETS

Pot du Crème is a flavored custard served in a small pot. These little pots are just enough—not quite large enough, some say—for one serving, and some have tiny lids. Orleanians delight in scooping a bit from someone else's serving, so the lid is an excellent accessory.

Café au lait at the French Market is a rich combination of chicory coffee and hot whole milk poured at the same time. It's served with a plate of warm New Orleans beignets, air-puffed square donuts, (ben-yeas, please) and dusted with powdered sugar. As special morning flavors, this dessert brings the day full circle to evening.

YIELD: 8 SERVINGS

CUSTARD RECIPE

3 cups	heavy whipping cream	3 tablespoons	strong coffee and chicory, or strong espresso, cold
1/2	vanilla bean split lengthwise	2 ounces	semi-sweet chocolate, melted, and cooled
1/4 cup	whole black coffee beans		
6 large	egg yolks, room temperature		
1/2 cup	granulated sugar	sprinkle	cocoa or espresso powder

Preheat the oven to 325°F.

Scrape the inside of the vanilla bean, and place both the husk, and seeds into the cream. Pour heavy whipping cream, and coffee beans into a saucepan. Place over medium-low heat. Bring the cream to a brief simmer (boiling will cause it to overflow). Remove from heat. Strain through a fine mesh sieve. Remove and discard the coffee beans and vanilla bean husk.

In a large bowl, whisk together the egg yolks, and sugar until the sugar dissolves, and the mixture is lemon-colored, approximately 3 minutes. Temper the yolks by gradually whisking the hot cream into the yolk and sugar mixture. Tempering means do not add the hot cream too quickly or the eggs will scramble. Stir in the brewed coffee and melted chocolate.

Pour the egg-cream mixture into eight 4-ounce Pot du Crème cups, ramekins or cappuccino cups, filling each cup until 3/4 full. Fill a large, shallow baking pan with 1/2 inch of warm water. Carefully place the filled cups in the water bath and bake for approximately 45 minutes. The centers should jiggle slightly when done. Remove the pan from the oven, and let the cups cool in the water for 10 minutes. When cooled, remove from water, and place them in the refrigerator to chill for at least 2 hours.

Serve topped with a swirled dollop of whipped cream, dust lightly with cocoa or espresso powder. Highlight with a trio of small beignets or other sweet treat. The whipped cream recipe is on page 33. The beignet recipe is on page 52.

NOTE: For advance preparation, cover the cups with plastic wrap, and refrigerate. Uncover and leave at room temperature for an hour before adding the garnishes, and serving.

Pot de Crème china courtesy of Elise Abrams Antiques

CANDIES &
COOKIES

Candy making is most assuredly an art, definitely a science, and an unbridled joy, especially the selection of ingredients. It can be genuinely unforgiving and requires accurate measurements, exact ingredients, timing, good equipment, temperature control, and patience.

Professionals do not make substitutions of main ingredients or take shortcuts. They also use the correct tools.

Invest in a good candy thermometer, dry and liquid measuring cups, measuring spoons and a 1- x 2 -foot (or larger if you prefer) slab of marble for cooling candy.

For safety's sake, keep children and pets away from the kitchen when boiling the candy. Scalding sugar sticks to the skin and causes extremely painful, dangerous burns.

For best results make candy during cool weather. Humidity or rain is an enemy of candy-making. The results can be disappointing.

Now cookie baking is not quite as intolerant as candy making, however it too requires self control. Save those creative urges for their decoration.

Always use the best ingredients you can budget.

Served with café au lait, or chocolate milk if you're a youngster, the experience of coffee and the donuts called beignets is so quintessentially New Orleans it is almost a cliché. Beignets are a custom with the added excitement of confectioners' sugar to puff toward your tablemates.

Many natives offer the empty seats at their table to visitors, treating them to an order of café au lait and beignets. It is our welcome to the city and an incentive to return for more sunny hospitality. It may be the bend in the river which cradles us and causes our quirky habits.

Locals swear by beignets as a hangover cure and prom dates never get home without a confectioners' sugar-dusted tuxedo. We are wary of children clutching a sugary handful of these goodies.

Beignets were named the Louisiana State donut in 1984.

BEIGNETS

Beignets are square fried donuts with no holes, liberally dusted with confectioners' sugar, and served daily at the French Market. Their origins are attributed to Africa, France, and the Celts. While no one seems to have bragging rights to actually creating beignets, many cultures have their own versions of fritters, fried pastry, and other donut-like treats. We claim beignets.

Some historians believe that the Ursuline Nuns of France brought the recipe to Louisiana when they arrived here in 1727. It is also believed that the beignet is the father of the raised donut.

Beignet, which is not much more than fried dough, may also be used to create canapés. The dough embraces fillings such as chocolate, custards or savories such as cheese or seafood stuffing. Simply roll out the dough a more thinly than directed, cut it into a rectangle, and gently fold it over the stuffing. Pinch the open edges together. Fry as a puff-filled canapé.

YIELD: 2 DOZEN 3-INCH BEIGNETS

1 package	active dry yeast (1/4-ounce)		pinch	salt
3/4 cup	warm water (110°F)		1 large	egg, beaten
1/4 cup	evaporated milk		4 to 4-1/4 cups	all-purpose flour
1 teaspoon	granulated sugar		1 quart	vegetable oil for frying
			1 cup	confectioners' sugar

Stir together yeast and 3/4 cup warm water in a 2-cup measuring cup. Let stand for 5 minutes. In a large bowl stir together yeast mixture, evaporated milk, sugar, salt, and egg until blended. Gradually stir in enough flour to make a soft dough. Cover the dough and chill for at least 8 hours.

Place chilled dough on a well-floured surface, and knead 5 or 6 times. Roll dough into a 15- x 15-inch shape, and cut into 3-inch squares. If preparing the miniature beignets called for in Chef John Besh's beignet recipe on page 48, cut them into 2-inch squares or smaller. Smaller beignets will puff and brown faster, so do not leave them unattended.

Pour oil to depth of 3 or 4 inches into a deep skillet or Dutch oven, and heat to 375°F. Using tongs, place each beignet into the hot oil. Working rapidly, fry several beignets at a time, not letting them touch, for approximately 1 minute on each side or until golden brown. Turn gently with tongs to brown each side evenly. Drain well on paper towels, and sprinkle warm beignets with confectioners' sugar.

Serve immediately, piping hot.

SISTER MARY
CLASSIC PRALINES

Legend tells us that pralines were named after Cesar du Plessis Praslin, a grand marshal of pre-Napoleonic France. It is said Praslin's cook, Clément Lassagne, coated his master's almonds with sugar to prevent indigestion.

The crown jewel of New Orleans' confections, there are as many praline recipes as there are bread pudding recipes. Everyone has a favorite. Sister Mary's pralines are fragile, sugary, and melt-in-your-mouth light. Her version of the recipe has been passed down through generations of nuns. Sister Mary's candies could be appropriately pronounced pray-leens, but we say praw-leens, otherwise, us locals will know you're not from around here.

YIELD: 5 DOZEN

1-pound	light brown sugar, box		pinch	salt
2-1/2 cups	granulated sugar		1/2 stick	margarine (2 ounces)
2-1/2 cups	whole milk		1 teaspoon	vanilla extract
2-1/2 cups	pecans, chopped (medium-sized)			(or maple if desired)

Combine light brown sugar, granulated sugar, milk, and salt in the pot. Cook on medium heat until the thermometer reaches 240°F, the soft-ball stage. Stir frequently to avoid sticking and burning. If the mixture sticks, scorches or burns, you must start over. To test, remove the pot from heat so it does not scorch and drop a small amount of mixture into cold water. The candy will form a soft, loose ball. If the soft ball stage has not been reached, return the pot to heat. Once the mixture has reached the proper soft-ball stage, remove from the heat and add the pecans, margarine, and pure vanilla or maple extract. Allow the candy to stand for 10 minutes without stirring.

Stir the mixture until the consistency is right for spooning (50 to 100 strokes). Spoon the pralines in a tablespoon size onto a marble slab or a sheet of waxed paper. Allow them to cool and dry. Lift each praline carefully using a spatula and turn it over to dry both sides.

Store in a tightly covered container or wrap individually.

NOTE: Sister Mary suggests using a cast-iron pot for the best results. This holds true for many recipes. Good cooks treasure cast-iron pots that have been passed down for generations. They can be found at garage sales, flea markets, second-hand shops or new at kitchen supply stores. The preferred brands seem to be Griswold or Lodge. New or rusted iron pots must be well scoured before use. Dry the pot thoroughly in a warm oven. Cool, then season it by wiping the pot liberally inside and out with vegetable oil. Heat slowly in the oven at 250°F for three hours. Once seasoned, clean the pot by wiping it out with a paper towel. Never immerse in water, or it must be re-seasoned.

CAUTION: Boiling sugar sticks to the skin and is extremely painful. Please take care.

© Photograph David G. Spielman

As early settlers of New Orleans in the 1700s nuns contributed mightily to the city's heritage and spiritual well-being.

They have provided cookery, medical care, gardening, education, and other charitable and religious services to the community. Nuns are credited with bringing the recipe for almond praline candy to New Orleans from France. Once here, they substituted the readily available pecans.

Today in an cloistered uptown convent surrounded by high brick walls and magnificent oak trees. The Poor Clare nuns share quiet, contemplative lives dedicated to poverty and prayer. Sister Mary makes and sells pralines as her part in sustaining the order. Visitors simply ring the convent bell. Sometimes the candies are available; at other times, they are not.

This recipe is Sister Mary's version, passed on to her from other members of the order.

Finding the colorful Roman-candy cart parked in the shade of a large oak tree is good luck and a delicious reason to stop for a treat with a nod to tradition. Ron Kottemann continues to use his great-grandmother's recipe to make her taffy.

The candy has always been cooked inside the cart. Ron's father and grandfather used a coal-burning stove. Today, Ron uses butane as the fuel. The original marble slab used for cooling the taffy, and the large hook for pulling the candy are still in use.

Patsy, the mule, ambles along, pulling her cart and taffy-making kitchen around the city, stopping in many different neighborhoods each day.

RON KOTTEMANN
ROMAN CHEWING CANDY

From an old Sicilian family recipe, the taffy we call Roman Chewing Candy dates back four generations to Angelina Napoli Cortese. Her son began making and selling her candy recipe in 1915 from a mule-drawn cart that he and wheelwright Tom Brinker designed. The cart is still in use. To make your own, plan an afternoon with the children or some strong teenagers for pulling the taffy.

YIELD: 24 STICKS

2 tablespoons	unsalted butter, at room temperature, plus extra for buttering your fingers during the pulling stage	1 tablespoon	distilled or cider vinegar
		1/4 teaspoon	salt
		1/4 teaspoon	baking soda
2 cups	granulated sugar	1 teaspoon flavorings	vanilla extract
2 tablespoons	cornstarch		chocolate extract
1 cup	light corn syrup		strawberry extract
3/4 cup	water, room temperature	food coloring	match flavorings

Butter a large marble slab or non-stick cookie sheet, and set aside.

In a large heavy saucepan, mix the sugar, and corn starch until combined. Add corn syrup, water, vinegar, butter, and salt. Stir over medium heat until sugar is dissolved and mixture comes to a boil. It is extremely important to remove any sugar crystals that stick to the sides of the pan by using a brush dipped in warm water. Otherwise, the entire mixture may recrystalize.

Clip a candy thermometer to the edge of the pan, and cook the mixture over medium heat until it comes to a boil and the temperature reaches 270°F, the soft crack stage. To test, remove the pot from the burner, so that the mixture does not overheat. Place a small drop of the mixture into cool water. It will solidify into threads that when removed from the water are flexible, not brittle. They will bend slightly before breaking. Do not stir the candy once it comes to a boil.

Stir in 1/4 teaspoon of baking soda. Divide into separate portions, and color and flavor each portion as desired in proportion to the size of each batch. Immediately pour the mixture onto the buttered marble. Place the candy in the coolest available spot in the kitchen.

When the taffy is cool enough to handle, wearing a pair of disposable rubber gloves, butter the gloves, and draw the taffy out into narrow ribbons. Double them back, and pull out again. Repeat the pulling and doubling over procedure a number of times. Pulling will get more difficult as it gets lighter in color and no longer sticky to the touch. Approximately 15 minutes is recommended. Pulling taffy incorporates tiny bubbles throughout the candy. This makes it lighter and chewier.

Divide into approximately 6 lumps, and pull each lump out until it is about 1/2 inch in diameter, and 2 feet long. Twist each pulled strip slightly, and using a pair of buttered scissors, cut it into 8-inch pieces. Braiding or twisting different colors together can create interesting effects. Wrap the candy in waxed paper, twisting the paper closed at each end.

NOTE: During cooking, the taffy is extremely hot and will cause painful burns. Keep children and pets out of the kitchen until the taffy has cooled enough to handle. Don't attempt to make taffy on rainy or humid days.

CHEF APRIL BELLOW
TUILE COOKIES

The fleur-de-lis, or flower of the lily, is an ancient graphic sign adopted by Louis II of France and embraced by New Orleans during his rule over the city. It is the city's symbol and our NFL football team logo. "Who dat? Who dat sez dey gonna beat dem Saints?"

YIELD: 12 to 18 COOKIES

5 tablespoons	unsalted butter, melted
2 large	egg whites
1/8 teaspoon	salt
1/3 cup	granulated sugar
1/2 teaspoon	vanilla extract
1/2 cup	all purpose flour
1/3 cup	pecans, finely chopped

Create your template the day prior to baking.

Preheat oven to 350°F.

In a large bowl sift the flour. Whisk together the melted butter, egg whites, and salt. Add sugar, vanilla extract, flour, and pecans, stirring until blended. Allow the batter to rest for at least 15 minutes. The batter may be spread evenly over a template or simply spooned onto baking parchment paper placed over a cookie sheet.

If using a template, place it on a baking parchment covered cookie sheet. Drop a tablespoon of the dough into the center of the open design. Using a cake knife, spread the dough to the edges of the design cavity, and level it out even with the cardboard template.

Using a toothpick trace around the design's inside edges to loosen the dough from the template. Lift, and repeat until the sheet is filled with cookies. An even consistency of the dough is important in order for the cookies to bake properly. Bake for 5 to 10 minutes, watching carefully. When they are golden brown remove them from the oven.

Allow to cool.

Drizzle with chocolate sauce, (recipe on page 90) or dust with confectioners' sugar, and use your creative inspiration to make the shape and decoration.

The template is the key to the cookie's shape. The process is exactly the opposite of using a cookie cutter. Rather than cutting the cookie out, this method fills it in. Select an open design.

Making a template is simple but requires planning, research and time. Begin the day prior to serving the cookies.

Cut a square of cardboard approximately 1 inch larger than the design.

Trace the design on a sheet of paper.

Lay the paper over a piece of cardboard as thick as the depth of your cookies. We used the cardboard backing from a legal pad.

Transfer the design by tracing over the paper, bearing down to indent the cardboard. If it is difficult to see the indentation, draw over it with a felt tip marker.

Cut out the cardboard's indented design with a sharp matte knife. Be careful.

Coat both sides of the cardboard with raw egg white to seal it. Allow to air dry completely. Flatten overnight under a stack of books.

A McKenzie's Bakery could be found on almost every corner. Spokesman Dick Bruce dubbed himself "The Old Pie Eater," and a grinning kid took a huge bite of the weekly special for the television commercials.

Owned by the Entringer family, the chain was closing when businessman Marc Leunissen, and his partners made a valiant, but futile effort to resurrect the bakeries.

Now, future generations of Orleanians will believe that turtles are slow-moving creatures properly eaten as soup.

Real turtles, the benchmark definitive kind, were a quickly consumed McKenzie's specialty–creamy milk chocolate generously swirled on a crumbly, confectioners' sugar dusted pecan cookie.

Longed for and certainly not forgotten.

MCKENZIE'S
TURTLE COOKIES

This recipe will take your taste buds back to a time when husbands would stop on their way home to pick up patty shells or a birthday cake. Office workers made a detour for morning donuts, and after school drop-ins for sweets were expressly forbidden. Although we never had more than a nickel or two in our pockets, it was enough for a turtle.

Turtles are still available around town at various bakeries. Some of them even place four pecans underneath the cookies as tiny feet, securing the pecans to the cookie with a dab of caramel. Cute. Nice. No matter how good they might be, they don't match a McKenzie-turtle memory.

YIELD: 36 COOKIES

1/2 stick	unsalted butter, room temperature (2 ounces)		1/3 cup	granulated sugar
			1 cup	pecans, chopped
2 teaspoons	vanilla extract		2 cups	all-purpose flour
2 teaspoons	water, room temperature		1/4 cup	confectioners' sugar

Preheat oven to 325°F.

Using an electric mixer, beat the room temperature butter for 30 seconds, until smooth and pale. Add the sugar, and continue beating until light and fluffy. Add 2 teaspoons of water, and the vanilla extract; beat well. Fold in the flour, and pecans. Shape into 1-inch balls and place on a non-stick or greased baking sheet. Bake for 20 minutes, then let cool. Otherwise, the warm cookies will melt the sugar. Place the confectioners' sugar in a plastic bag, and add the cookies. Shake gently to coat them.

CHOCOLATE BUTTER CREAM ICING

2-1 ounce squares	unsweetened chocolate		1 cup	whole milk
			4 tablespoons	unsalted butter
2-1 ounce squares	semi-sweet chocolate		4 cups	confectioners' sugar

In the top of a double boiler, combine both chocolates, milk, and butter. Place over medium heat, and stir occasionally until the chocolate has melted. Remove from the heat, and add the confectioners' sugar. Whisk with a fork until smooth. Refrigerate the icing for one hour, to firm.

Using a pastry bag, pipe chocolate swirls onto cooled, sugar dusted cookies. In lieu of a pastry bag, drop a generous teaspoon of frosting on each cookie. Refrigerate covered until ready to serve.

LINDA ELLERBEE
WEDDING MERINGUE KISSES

Meringue kisses are bite-sized clouds that dissolve on the tongue, and just one kiss is never enough. To form the kiss, two pieces of a baked meringue-like candy are married, using butter-cream icing. Chocolate is exquisite, vanilla subtle, and lemon or lime sweetly tart.

Meringue was traditionally a winter treat in New Orleans. Hot, humid summers prevented the dessert from setting up properly; however, with air conditioning, it is made, and enjoyed all year.

YIELD: 24 PAIR OF MERINGUES

4 large	egg whites
8 ounces	superfine sugar
1/8 teaspoon	cream of tartar
1 cup	buttercream icing

Preheat the oven to 200°F.

Using an electric mixer and a very clean, chilled, medium sized mixing bowl, beat the egg whites until they have almost reached the soft peak stage. Gradually add the sugar and cream of tartar in a slow, steady stream while you continue to beat the whites until they reach the firm peak stage.

When the mixture is stiff and glossy, place it in a piping bag with a star nozzle. Squeeze out little rosettes (about 1-1/2 to 2 inches in diameter) onto a cookie sheet lined with non-stick baking parchment.

Place the meringues in the oven for 20 to 30 minutes. Do not allow them to brown. If they begin to brown, turn off the oven and allow them to continue to cook using the residual heat. Test a meringue with the tip of your finger for firmness. It should be firm but soft to the touch. Once removed from the oven they will continue to harden as they cool.

CHOCOLATE BUTTERCREAM ICING

2-1 ounce squares	unsweetened chocolate	1 cup	whole milk
2-1 ounce squares	semi-sweet chocolate	4 tablespoons	unsalted butter
		4 cups	confectioners' sugar

In the top of a double boiler, combine both chocolates, milk, and butter. Place over medium heat and stir occasionally until the chocolate has melted. Remove from the heat, and add the confectioners' sugar. Whisk with a fork until smooth. Refrigerate the icing for one hour to firm.

When the meringues are cool, take one in your hand and with icing, wed it to the flat side of another meringue. Continue until all the meringues have a mate. Humidity wreaks havoc with the meringue, so try to serve immediately. Otherwise, place in a tightly covered container and refrigerate. They will keep for four or five days, if there are any left to store.

Linda Ellerbee is an honorary Orleanian, who lived with a benign ghost in a Jackson Square Pontalba apartment when she wrote her first best seller "And So It Goes."

She returns often to wander through the French Quarter, explore restaurants, and dine with friends. Cooking is one of her great pleasures, exceeded only by the appreciation of a fine meal prepared by someone else.

As an Orleanian habit, we adopt recipes from other countries and adapt them to our tastes. This one was readily embraced, and continues to be a favorite.

She got this recipe from Mary Brunner, a caterer in Llanidloes, Wales, who prepared it for the rehearsal dinner preceding Linda's son's wedding there. It was a three-day spectacular that began with a candle accidentally setting fire to the bride's hair the night before the wedding, and it concluded with a fireworks show staged over the rolling hills of Wales the night of the wedding.

Linda published Mary's version in another best seller, Take Big Bites: Adventures Around the World and Across the Table. *Linda continues to tinker with the recipe, which is her nature.*

Marcelle Bienvenu has done it all in the culinary world. Born in St. Martinville, La., she has worked with Commander's Palace, K-Paul's Louisiana Kitchen in New Orleans, and Brennan's of Houston. From 1981-1984, she owned and operated her own restaurant, Chez Marcelle, near Lafayette, La. Now she uses her food knowledge to write about what she's been eating.

Her resulting "Who's Your Mama, Are You Catholic and Can You Make a Roux" is a Cajun/Creole family album and cookbook from the bayou country. She coauthored, with Emeril Lagasse, Louisiana Real & Rustic, Emeril's Creole Christmas, Emeril's TV Dinners, and Everyday's a Party. She also contributed to Emeril Primetime, From Emeril's Kitchens, Emeril's Potluck, and Emeril's Delmonico: A Restaurant With a Past.

She edited the 1987 edition of the The Picayune's Creole Cook Book, originally published in 1901 and reissued to celebrate the newspaper's 150th anniversary. She also writes a weekly column for the paper.

Marcelle's home is a fine place to pass a good time around the kitchen table. There's nothing better than a good meal, laughter, and rollicking fun in Acadiana.

MARCELLE BIENVENU
Oreilles de Cochon

Marcelle says that oreilles de cochon means "pig's ears". They are a Cajun country treat, an example of purely making do with what is on hand, and turning it into something remarkable. Add a sprinkle of chopped pecans once the pig's ears have been dipped in cane syrup, so they are both sweet and crunchy.

YIELD: APPROXIMATELY 1 DOZEN PASTRIES

1 cup	all-purpose flour	1 can	Steen's® cane syrup
1/4 teaspoon	salt		(12 ounces)
about 1/2 cup	water, room	1/2 cup	pecans, finely chopped
as needed	temperature		vegetable oil for frying

In a medium bowl combine flour and salt. Mix thoroughly. Stir in enough water to make a stiff dough. Divide dough into 12 equal parts, and roll each into a ball. Roll out each of the small balls of dough on a lightly floured surface.

Pour about 2 inches of vegetable oil into a heavy, deep-frying pot. Heat the oil to 350°F.

Drop one of the balls into the hot oil. Using a long handled fork, stick the tines of the fork into the center of it and twist quickly. Hold fork in place until dough sets and holds the shape. This will give the appearance of a pig's ear. Cook until golden brown then drain well on paper towels. Repeat this procedure with the remaining small balls of dough.

In a heavy saucepan bring the cane syrup to a boil. Stir until the syrup reaches 240°F, the soft ball stage At this temperature a small amount of syrup dropped into cold water will form a soft, loose ball. Remove from heat.

Dip each pig's ear into the hot syrup, coating well. Sprinkle with chopped pecans, and lay on waxed paper. Serve warm or at room temperature. The pig's ears may be stored for one or two days. Separate, and place in a tightly sealed container.

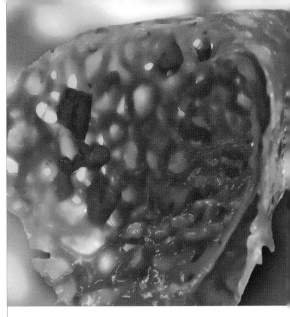

CHEF APRIL BELLOW
PECAN LACE COOKIES

A New Orleans' version of almond lace cookies, these will make your taste buds sing and dance. They are an airy, crunchy tidbit, and a new version of a classic.

Pecan Lace cookies are not your normal cookie; when warm they are flexible. When you take them out of the oven you can make fluted dessert cups by gently pressing the warm cookies over a small upturned bowl, or ice cream cones by using a glass, or tightly rolled in pencil shapes to garnish a dessert. Of course, you can serve them flat. But why?

YIELD: APPROXIMATELY 12 – 6" CIRCLES

1/2 cup	pecans, finely chopped	1/2 stick	unsalted butter, softened
1/3 cup	all-purpose flour		(2 ounces)
1/2 cup	light brown sugar, packed	1/4 cup	light corn syrup

Preheat oven to 350°F.

In a small bowl combine the pecans and flour. Set it aside.

Using a small, heavy saucepan, combine the butter, sugar, and light corn syrup. Bring to a boil. Remove from heat and stir in the pecans and flour mixture. Transfer the batter to a bowl and stir occasionally until it thickens into a dough and is cool enough to handle, approximately 30 minutes.

With moistened hands, roll the dough into various size balls, depending on whether you're making cookies, cups, garnish, or coronets. Place on ungreased baking sheets, 3 to 7 inches apart, depending on size. They spread quite a bit. Bake for approximately 8 to 10 minutes, or until the active bubbling subsides.

Place the baking sheet on a cooling rack for approximately 1 minute until the cookies are firm enough to lift with a flexible metal spatula. The cookies remain malleable for 3 to 5 minutes. Working quickly, mold each into desired shape and set on a wire rack to cool completely. Once cooled, the cookies are brittle, so handle with care. If the cookies become too brittle to mold, place the tray back in the oven for a minute to soften.

If using a baking sheet more than once, allow it to cool. Wipe off the excess butter with a paper towel before dropping the next batch of batter.

Family and friends tested the initial recipes before we were ready for a professional shakedown. Our official and most critical test cook in the home kitchen was April Bellow, a young chef at Arnaud's, who worked on her days off and before her shift at the restaurant.

April graduated from Johnson & Wales University's culinary arts program following an internship at Arnaud's. She returned to Arnaud's and continues to learn, working with Executive Chef Tommy DiGiovanni and Pastry Chef Cathy Pollard.

An experienced cook, but not a baker, she knows her way around a kitchen, but a lot of this was new to her, too. Chef Cathy's advice and occasional guffaws cheered us onward.

The real fun was playing "what if," and April always bit. Nothing intimidated her.

The classic version of this cookie recipe uses almonds, but April substituted pecans–an inspiration of a young chef in the finest New Orleans tradition.

April's Pecan Lace cookies are terrific for ice cream cones, side surprises for other desserts, and just good eating.

FLAMBÉ

Bonfires along the levee above New Orleans light the way for Papa Noel each Christmas Eve. The festive blazes signal that Christmas is here, and the bonfires precede the New Year's Eve fireworks over the Mississippi. Flames are enchanting at any time of the year, and even more so at a dessert table.

Flambé is French for "flaming" or "flamed." A liquor, usually brandy, cognac, or rum, is warmed from below the bowl of a long metal ladle then lit with a long match. The alcohol flames, leaving behind the faint essence of the liquor or liqueur. The flaming alcohol is then carefully poured over a dessert for dramatic flair.

Only liquors or liqueurs with a high alcohol content of at least 40 percent, or 80-proof will burn for flambés, and the higher the alcohol content, the more readily they will ignite. Do not use any alcohol above 60 percent or 120-proof.

Vigorously shaking the pan usually extinguishes the flame, but keep a kitchen fire extinguisher or pot lid nearby to smother the flames if they get out of control. The alcohol burns off in a matter of seconds but if the flames catch anything else nearby, there will be trouble.

There are strict rules for safe flambé-cooking. Never add liquor to the flambé pan while it is over the flame. Always flame the liquor in a ladle, and then pour the flaming contents into the pan.

Avoid flambé around draperies, upholstery, near the guests' hair and clothing, or below an intake vent.

Please be careful.

Antoine's is treasured for quirky local habits, a private Orleanians' entrance and personal waiters. It is America's oldest restaurant and is still operated by the same family that founded it.

Baked Alaska is one of the most famous celebration desserts, and it is fitting that Antoine's version highlights the holidays.

During the mid-1800s, Creole families celebrated a Réveillon dinner twice during the season. The first was on Christmas Eve, and the follow-up was New Year's Eve, with a second and even more festive Réveillon repast.

New Orleans restaurants present a special once-a-year Réveillon menu throughout the holiday season, celebrated from December 1 through 23. Now everyone may share our traditions in the spirit of the past.

TIP: Depending on your creative instincts, decorative hearts, swans or flowers may be piped on a sheet of baking parchment, using meringue in a pastry bag fitted with the appropriate nozzle. Prepare these flourishes in advance and harden them in a preheated 200°F oven for 1/2 hour then set aside for use as decorations. Decorations may also be purchased and we won't tell anyone that they are not homemade.

ANTOINE'S
BAKED ALASKA

A beautiful bombe (upside down bowl) shape is slathered with toasted meringue dressed with fancy meringue swans and ceremoniously brought to the table. The waiter who pours a ladle of flaming brandy over it administers the coupe de grâce. The shape, of course, is a matter of preference. Advance planning is the key to Baked Alaska. The dessert must be organized the day prior to serving. Prepare decorative garnishes ahead of time.

YIELD: 12 SERVINGS

9 inch	sponge cake, 1 layer	6 tablespoons	granulated sugar
1 quart	ice cream, any flavor	2 tablespoons	brandy for flaming
3 large	egg whites, room temperature	garnish	chocolate sauce
			meringue decorations
1/2 teaspoon	fresh lemon juice		long fireplace matches

The night before soften the ice cream at room temperature until it is easily scooped. Choose a 1-quart metal mixing bowl that is 1 inch smaller in diameter than the sponge cake, and pack the ice cream firmly into the bowl, smoothing the top. Re-freeze overnight, until completely solid. Refrigerate the cake.

At least 45 minutes before the dessert is to be served, place the sponge cake on a large, heatproof platter. Loosen the ice cream from its metal bowl by plunging the bowl into a bath of hot water for five seconds. Quickly invert the bowl on top of the sponge cake until it releases. Return the platter to the freezer while you prepare the meringue.

Place the oven rack at the lowest level and preheat the broiler.

In a very clean, chilled, medium mixing bowl, beat the egg whites and lemon juice until they have almost reached the soft peak stage. Gradually add the sugar in a slow, steady stream while you continue to beat the whites until they reach the firm peak stage.

Remove the cake and ice cream from the freezer. Working quickly, use a rubber spatula to coat the dome of ice cream and the cake base completely with meringue, swirling to create a wavy surface.

Place the platter under the broiler for 2 to 3 minutes until the peaks of meringue turn a pale golden brown. If necessary, turn once or twice for even browning. Watch constantly. Do not leave this arrangement unattended even for a moment. It will either burn, melt or both.

Quickly pipe a meringue edge around the base of the dome. With skill, a name or date may be written in meringue on the dome at the last minute. Add any previously piped decorations to the top or sides.

Warm the brandy and proceed directly to the table. Pour the warmed brandy into a prewarmed, large ladle and light it with a long match. Drizzle the flaming brandy all around the edge of the Baked Alaska and scoop individual portions into bowls.

Serve with chocolate sauce as an accoutrement in a gravy boat. The recipe is on page 90.

NOTE: Please use extreme caution when flaming a dish. A fire extinguisher must be nearby.

© Photograph Paul Rico

BANANAS FOSTER

Just about everyone has heard of Breakfast at Brennan's, a brunch extravaganza. Fewer people know that 25¢ martinis attracted the advertising industry lunch crowd during the '70s and '80s. Media salespeople would table-hop, collecting orders and tapes from advertising agency executives who also dined there. Afternoons at the media outlets and advertising agencies were slow, sleepy times or occasions of grandiosity and peculiar decisions. Entire afternoons could be lost.

So is the 25¢ martini.

Brennan's Restaurant brought this old Creole dish to prominence when the recipe was revised, ladled over vanilla ice cream, and named for a favored guest. At breakfast, lunch or dinner, a grand finale of Bananas Foster adds more than a sparkle in the event.

YIELD: 6 SERVINGS

6 teaspoons	ground cinnamon	1/3 cup	dark rum
1 tablespoon	granulated sugar	1/4 cup	Creme de Banana
6 tablespoons	unsalted butter (3 ounces)		(banana liqueur)
3 cups	light brown sugar	6 scoops	vanilla ice cream,
6 whole	bananas, peeled, halved		slightly softened
	lengthwise and quartered		long fireplace matches

In a small bowl, combine the cinnamon, and sugar, mix thoroughly, and set aside.

In a flambé pan or a chafing dish, combine the butter and brown sugar. Mash together, then place the pan over medium heat. Stir with a wooden spoon until the sugar melts and the mixture caramelizes to a creamy, rich brown color. This process requires approximately 5 minutes.

Add the banana pieces to the pan, cut sides down and cook for approximately 1 minute. Place the rum in a large prewarmed ladle and ignite with a long match. Drizzle the flaming rum into the pan.

Scatter the cinnamon-sugar mixture directly over the flame. As the flames die, pour the banana liqueur into a large, prewarmed metal ladle and ignite with a long match. Drizzle the flaming banana liqueur into the pan and stir gently to combine all the ingredients. The flames will quickly go out.

Immediately place one scoop of ice cream in each of six saucer style champagne glasses or bowls. Spoon some of the banana mixture on top, and plenty of the pan juices. Serve immediately.

VARIATIONS: Substitute any soft fruit for this dish that has a correspondingly flavored liqueur—peaches, pears, apricots or berries.

NOTE: Please use extreme caution when flaming a dish. A fire extinguisher must be nearby.

Money does grow on trees in the Big Easy.

From founder Owen Brennan's strong roots a forest of restaurants has grown—at least a thicket. The large, unwieldy family has opened one establishment after another, enlisting their children, cousins, and other family members.

Owen established Brennan's in its current location on Royal Street in 1954. The restaurant is in a historic Vieux Carré building and dependency.

The original carriage way has been converted to the restaurant's grand entry with a sweeping stairway, and leads to an extravagant, lush tropical courtyard. It is complete with banana trees.

Various flags have flown over Louisiana, most notably Spanish and then French. A significant part of our more refined culinary heritage comes courtesy of French cooking.

Cherries Jubilee was created to honor Queen Victoria's Golden Jubilee, the fiftieth year of her reign, by French Chef Auguste Escoffier.

This elegant, majestic dessert has been featured and flamed in many of New Orleans' restaurants but it has become a rarity on menus.

Flambéd at the table it creates a spectacular gesture for a gala celebration.

Cherries are in season from the end of May through August, hitting their peak around the 4th of July. Short but sweet. At other times, they are probably imported, if they can be found at all. Canned or frozen cherries make an acceptable substitute.

We don't know why September 24 is Cherries Jubilee Day, when they are out of season. Who decides these things?

BROUSSARD'S
CHERRIES JUBILEE

Chef Gunter Preuss with Evelyn, his wife, created another of New Orleans restaurant families when they acquired and restored Broussard's Restaurant in the French Quarter. Their son Marc now presides over the lovely establishment, founded in 1920, which opens to a grand Vieux Carré patio. Chef Preuss served Cherries Jubilee when he wished to mark a special occasion. Marc carries on the tradition.

YIELD: 6 SERVINGS

2 pounds	fresh cherries, pits removed, or substitute with	1 quart	vanilla ice cream
2 cans	dark sweet cherries, 32 ounces, drained; liquid reserved	2 tablespoons	Cherry Herring, Cherry Marnier or another sweet cherry brandy/liqueur
		2 tablespoons	cognac for flaming long fireplace matches

Drain cherries, reserving the liquid. In a large bowl, mash 1 cup of cherries with liquid. Combine with drained cherries in a saucepan over low heat. Pour liquid in with cherries, and heat until reduced by half. Pour the cherry liqueur in with the cherries and stir.

Carefully pour the brandy into a large, prewarmed metal ladle, and light with a long fireplace match. Pour the flaming brandy over the cherries. Allow blue flame to burn off and immediately spoon cherry mixture over vanilla ice cream.

NOTE: Please use extreme caution when flaming a dish. A fire extinguisher must be nearby.

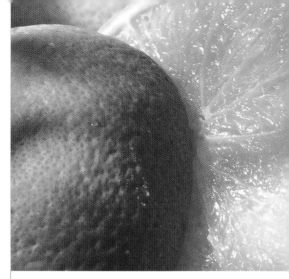

CHEF GAETANO DIGIOVANNI
Crêpes Suzette Arnaud

Crêpes Suzette Arnaud is a personal favorite that proprietor Archie Casbarian reintroduced to his restaurant's menu when he acquired and revitalized the historic establishment. Coincidentally, Crêpes Suzette Arnaud appeared on the restaurant's mid '30s menus.

YIELD: SERVES 6, 12 CRÊPES

1 cup	whole milk	1 teaspoon	vegetable oil
1 large	egg	1 cup	all-purpose flour, sifted
1/4 teaspoon	Kosher or sea salt		vegetable oil for frying

Prepare the crêpes ahead of time or use prepared frozen crêpes. Before serving, warm 6 plates in a low temperature oven for 15 minutes. In a blender, combine the milk, egg, salt, oil, and flour. Blend until smooth. The batter should be about the thickness of heavy whipping cream; if you prefer thinner, more delicate crêpes, add a little more milk a few teaspoons at a time, until the batter is the consistency of half-and-half. Cover and let the batter rest in the refrigerator for 30 minutes.

Wipe a small non-stick frying pan (5- to 7- inches in diameter) with a paper towel that has been moistened with vegetable oil. Place the pan over medium-high heat. If the pan is hot enough, the batter will make a hissing noise when poured into the skillet. Use a 1-ounce ladle to pour the batter for the first crêpe into the center of the pan. Immediately lift the pan from the heat and tilt and swirl it, to coat the base of the pan with a thin, even layer of batter. Return the pan to the heat. Lower the heat to medium after cooking a few crêpes, or they will cook too quickly, toughen, and burn.

After a minute or so, when the crêpe turns brown at the edges, gently loosen with a spatula, and flip it over. Cook the remaining side until any moisture disappears, only another minute or so. Transfer the finished crêpe to a lightly oiled plate, and make the remaining crêpes in the same way, wiping the pan with the oiled towel again as necessary. Cover the stack of crêpes with a paper towel and cool to room temperature. If desired, cover with plastic wrap and refrigerate for up to 24 hours before using.

SUZETTE

12	prepared crêpes	1/4 cup	brandy
1/2 stick	unsalted butter (2 ounces)	1/2 lemon	juice
1 cup	granulated sugar		thin slices of lemon for garnish
1 teaspoon	grated orange zest	1 orange	juice
1 teaspoon	grated lemon zest		thin slices of orange for garnish
1/2 cup	Grand Marnier® liqueur		long fireplace matches

In a flambé pan or chafing dish, combine the butter, and sugar. Place over medium heat, and stir until the butter has melted, and the sugar has dissolved. Add the lemon and the orange zest, and carefully stir until slightly caramelized, and golden (do not leave the pan unattended during this step). Add the Grand Marnier®, orange and lemon juices and stir together.

Add the crêpes 2 at a time, and simmer for about 30 seconds on each side, until warmed. Fold the crêpes into halves then quarters (the finished shape is triangular), and baste with the pan juices. Repeat this process for each crêpe.

Pour the brandy into a large, prewarmed metal ladle, and ignite with a long match. Drizzle the flaming brandy over the crêpes, and serve as soon as the flames die. Garnish each plate with a paper thin slice each of orange, lemon, slivers, and zest.

NOTE: Please use extreme caution when flaming a dish. A fire extinguisher must be nearby.

Arnaud's Executive Chef Tommy DiGiovanni is a native Orleanian, esteemed Delgado Culinary Arts graduate, and chef whose inventiveness represents the epitome of classic Creole, French and Italian cooking. He began his career as a line cook at Arnaud's.

He has worked with the best in the culinary world and received numerous accolades and awards for his creativity.

When he returned to Arnaud's as executive chef, he was greeted with a banner emblazoned "Welcome Home, Tommy" and applause from his crew. As executive chef, he serves royalty, presidents, and super stars.

Crêpes Suzette were created either at the Café de Paris in Monte Carlo or at La Maison Française in Rockefeller Center, circa 1896, then popularized in America by Henri Charpentier, the French-born chef. One legend says Charpentier devised the dish in honor of a beautiful lady named Suzette who accompanied Edward, Prince of Wales II, to the Café de Paris.

Another tale has the dish named to acknowledge a well-known courtesan. Prince Edward denied ever having known a woman named Suzette. Yet Edward ordered Crêpes Suzette at London's Savoy. He said "a single taste would reform a cannibal into a civilized gentleman."

Whether or not the stories are true, they make a fitting garnish when serving this decadent dessert.

ICES &
ICE CREAM

Strawberries and blueberries grow in abundance across Lake Pontchartrain. Dewberries hide under prickly bushes. Sweet peaches blush. Sugar cane fields lie downriver from the city. Nearby in Plaquemines Parish, groves of pecan trees overhang the road from either side, creating a cool green corridor mottled with sunshine that seems to lead to another time. It does lead to acres of citrus and other fruit farms.

Located just minutes from downtown are quiet places of contrasts. Generations of farmers have cultivated the fruits and vegetables that grace Orleanians' tables. A visit to a farmer's stand or a stop at a roadside truck is a delightful excuse to choose the season's best and freshest produce.

Not only fruits and berries are used for ice creams and ices. Many flavors are possible using herbs or candies, with the ice base of simple syrup, or ice cream's vanilla custard base.

For example, devotees of peppermint ice cream here were frustrated by supply and demand. More demand than supply. Are peppermints in season only during the holidays?

Stephen K. Bellaire, CPA, thinks about these dilemmas and found an answer. He makes his own by simply crushing peppermints and stirring them into excellent vanilla ice cream, then refreezes it.

Only a few people would go to that length, but then again, he likes peppermint ice cream and so does Sheila, his wife. She seeks the finest candies for his recipe. That's her part of the job. Add chocolate sauce and it's a wonderful treat or gift for any season.

How could you resist such an excellent reason to get out the ice cream freezer? You know the one, it was probably a present and is in the back of the cabinet.

ANGELO BROCATO'S®
CANTALOUPE ICE

As rich in history as it is in flavor, Angelo Brocato's® Original Italian Ice Cream and Confectionery is a time-honored New Orleans tradition. The cheerful old-fashioned shop is operated by the third generation of the Brocato family, led by Arthur Brocato.

They are most famous for their seasonal fresh fruit ices and spumoni ice cream, in addition to Italian pastries, sweets and cookies. An afternoon stop or after-dinner drop in at the ice cream parlor for an ice, gelato, or cannoli is a popular excursion and an opportunity to visit with the Brocato clan.

YIELD: 2 QUARTS

1 quart	water, (8 cups)	1 lemon	juiced
2-1/2 cups	granulated sugar	2 medium	cantaloupes, ripened

To make the basic simple syrup, dissolve sugar and water in a 2 quart saucepan over medium-high heat. Bring to a boil and cook for 2 minutes. Remove from the heat and cool.

Peel and seed the cantaloupes. Cut into 2-inch pieces. Puree in a food processor. Strain through a medium sieve. Mix strained cantaloupe juice, sugar syrup, and lemon juice with a wire whisk.

Pour into an ice cream machine to churn and freeze it according to the manufacturer's directions. Add some cantaloupe pulp, if desired.

Freeze to a smooth consistency.

Pack the cantaloupe ice into a covered container and place the ice into the freezer for a few hours to harden completely.

Serving suggestion: Serve in a dessert glass topped with whipped cream or with a scoop of vanilla ice cream. Garnish with fresh mint leaves.

As spring turns into summer Orleanians move a little slower. It usually rains each afternoon, cooling sidewalks and watering the plants. Palmettos and banana trees shade lawns and courtyards.

Crêpe Myrtle trees burst into bloom overnight. The streets become splashed with magenta, purple, lavender, and pale pink as the trees drop their blossoms, reminding us of Brocato's ices and sno-ball syrup's vivid colors.

The birth of the New Orleans sno-ball evolved from George Ortolano's 1936 invention SnoWizard®, a machine that created finely shaved, fluffy ice snow and a brand new industry. Sno-ball stands across the city open each summer.

When we can't get to Brocato's we make ices and sorbets at home. It's so simple that there is no excuse not to get out the ice cream machine. Remember where you put it?

Executive Chef Susan Spicer is as generous as she is talented, benefitting numerous organizations through her extraordinary culinary efforts.

Her trademark bandana has been behind the stoves of some of the city's most illustrious and the world's most prestigious kitchens. Spicer's innovative take on Big Easy flavors spiked with international accents has brought her to prominence. She was named as Best Chef, Southeast, by the James Beard Foundation. Her accolades and awards are numerous.

Bayona was founded in 1990 by Susan Spicer and Regina Keever. It's cool, lush patio is tucked behind a 200-year-old Creole cottage and dependency on rue Dauphine, the original Spanish name Camino de Bayona.

PEACH MELBA ICE CREAM SANDWICH

Louisiana's peaches from Plaquemines Parish and Ruston are treasures and provide the basis for this recipe with a twist and a grin from Executive Chef Susan Spicer's Bayona. Legendary Chef Auguste Escoffier created Peach Melba in 1894 at the Savoy Hotel to toast diva Dame Nellie Melba following her performance of the opera *Lohengrin* at London's Covent Garden. New Orleans' cooks shamelessly adopted it almost immediately, as we do most good things.

YIELD: 4 SERVINGS ROASTED PEACHES

2	peaches, peeled, halved, and pitted	1/4 cup	brown sugar
		1/4 cup	Steen's® cane syrup
		splash	Chambord® liqueur

Preheat the oven to 375°F.

In a bowl, toss the peaches with the brown sugar and cane syrup. Spread the peaches on a non-stick baking sheet, and roast for 8 to 10 minutes, until slightly caramelized. Remove from the oven, and cool.

YIELD: 8 CINNAMON COOKIES

2 sticks	butter (8 ounces)	2-3/4 cups	all-purpose flour
1/2 cup	granulated sugar	1/4 cup	almond meal (ground almonds)
1/4 teaspoon	salt	2 teaspoons	ground cinnamon
1 large	egg	extra sugar	for dusting
1/2 teaspoon	vanilla extract	1 pint	vanilla ice cream
		1/4 cup	raspberry jam

In a standing mixer fitted with the paddle attachment, cream together the butter, sugar, and salt until fluffy. Mix in the egg and vanilla, scraping down the sides of the mixing bowl with a rubber spatula. Combine the flour, almond meal, and cinnamon mixing until just combined. Wrap the dough in plastic wrap and chill for 1 hour in refrigerator.

Preheat oven to 325°F.

Unwrap the cookie dough, and place on a sheet of parchment paper. Lightly flour the top of the dough and roll it out to 1/4-inch thickness. Using a 2-1/2 inch round cutter, cut 8 circles from the dough, without removing them. Refrigerate the parchment sheet for 30 minutes. Place another piece of parchment paper on a baking sheet. Remove the circles from the dough, and place them on a parchment-lined pan. Dust the tops with a little granulated sugar. Bake for approximately 10 to 15 minutes, until slightly golden brown. Remove from oven, and cool completely on a cookie rack.

Turn all of the cookies upside down and spread a little raspberry jam on each. Place a small scoop of vanilla ice cream on four of the cookies. Place a roasted peach half on top of each scoop of ice cream. Finish by topping the peaches with the remaining cookies, jam side down, drizzle with Chambord® , and serve immediately. Bayona's recipe for vanilla ice cream is on page 85.

MILE HIGH ICE CREAM PIE

Albert Aschaffenberg is a true gentleman who presided over the Pontchartrain Hotel and its now-extinct Caribbean Room, prior to his retirement. Well known for his gracious hospitality and cultured manner, he and his late chef Louis Evans created one of New Orleans' most spectacular desserts and introduced it in 1948. Miss Annie Laurie was the beloved pastry cook responsible for its making. Mile High Pie is appropriately named and towers over almost any other sweet. Locals tiptoeing out of the hotel have not been naughty; they've merely stopped for a piece of Mile High Pie to break their diets. It is now served in the hotel's Café Pontchartrain.

YIELD: 9-INCH PIE

CRUST:

1-1/4 cup	unbleached, all-purpose flour	5 tablespoons	salted butter, cold, cut into small pieces	
1 tablespoon	granulated sugar	4 tablespoons	water, ice	
2 tablespoons	vegetable shortening	1	ovenproof plastic bag filled with pennies	

FILLING:

1 pint	vanilla ice cream	8 large	egg whites
1 pint	chocolate ice cream	1/2 teaspoon	vanilla extract
1 pint	peppermint or strawberry ice cream	1/4 teaspoon	cream of tartar
		1/2 cup	granulated sugar

Combine flour and sugar with a fork or whisk. Add shortening and butter, combine thoroughly using a pastry cutter until mixture resembles coarse crumbs. Fold ice water into previous mixture and bring dough together by hand, kneading until smooth. Form the dough into a disk shape, wrap and refrigerate for at least 1 hour.

Preheat oven to 400° F.

Remove dough from refrigerator and bring to room temperature (about 15 minutes). Prepare work area by sprinkling flour on the surface of the table and on the rolling pin. Roll the dough out to about 1/8 of an inch. Drape the dough over the rolling pin and center it over a Pyrex pie plate. Gently adjust the dough so that it lays flat in the pie plate. Leaving about 2 inches from the edge of the tin, trim excess dough using shears or a knife. Fold excess under and create desired edge by pinching with fingers or pressing with a fork. Place the bag of pennies into the pie shell. The entire bottom of the pie shell should be weighted. Bake the pie shell for approximately 20 minutes. Remove from oven when golden brown, remove pennies, and allow the shell to cool before proceeding.

Layer slightly softened ice cream in the pie shell and return to freezer. Beat the egg whites with the vanilla and cream of tartar until soft peaks form. Gradually add 1/2 cup of sugar, beating until the egg whites are stiff and glossy and the sugar has dissolved. Remove the pie and spread the meringue over the ice cream to the edges of the pastry.

Set the freezer temperature as cold as possible. Freeze the pie for at least several hours. Prepare the chocolate sauce and reheat it just before serving.

Remove pie from the freezer and place under a preheated broiler for 30 seconds to 1 minute to brown the meringue, or use a butane torch designed for such delicate undertakings. Serve immediately.

CHOCOLATE SAUCE

6 squares	German sweet chocolate (6 ounces)
6 squares	unsweetened chocolate (6 ounces)
1-1/2 cups	granulated sugar
1-1/2 cups	heavy whipping cream

To prepare the hot chocolate sauce put the chocolates, 1-1/2 cups of granulated sugar, and 3/4 cup of heavy whipping cream in the top of a double boiler. Cook until the sauce is melted and thick. Add the balance of the cream to achieve a pouring consistency. Drizzle the hot chocolate sauce over each serving.

LEMON ICE

Following a meal, between courses or as a pick-me-up, lemon ice is a sweet, spiked with citrus. It is one of Brocato's® most heralded specialties. The recipe is a family secret, however, our taste tests against the Brocato® original say that this one is especially close.

YIELD: 1 QUART

1 cup	fresh lemon juice	1-1/4 cup	granulated sugar
1 teaspoon	grated lemon zest	1-1/4 cup	water, cold

In a small saucepan, combine the sugar and water and boil until the sugar is absorbed completely, to make a simple syrup. Place the lemon juice, zest, and simple syrup in the bowl of an ice cream freezer and churn for 20 to 25 minutes or until frozen. Pack into covered container and place in the freezer to harden completely. For garnish use fresh mint leaves, a curl of lemon rind, lemon zest, or brightly colored berries.

WATERMELON ICE

Food processors and the electric ice cream maker have made watermelon ice an easy recipe, but that wasn't always the case. Pulling the bowl from the freezer to periodically stir the concoction was time consuming. It is delicious, however. The taste memory lingers, as does a perfect summer day.

YIELD: 1 QUART

4 cups	watermelon, seeded and cubed	1/3 cup	granulated sugar
1/2 cup	water, cold	1 tablespoon	fresh lemon juice

Place watermelon in blender or food processor and puree until smooth. In a small saucepan, combine the sugar and water and boil until the sugar is absorbed completely, to make a simple syrup. Sugar may be adjusted according to the sweetness of the watermelon. Combine all ingredients and churn in the bowl of an ice cream freezer for 20 to 25 minutes or until frozen. Pack into covered container and place in the freezer to harden completely.

NOTE: For a fluffier ice, sometimes called a sorbet, whip two egg whites into stiff meringue peaks. At the conclusion of the first freezing, fold carefully into the ice mixture then replace in the freezer to harden.

GINNY WARREN
STRAWBERRY ICE

It's not possible in New Orleans to exclude strawberry ice as a delicious recipe to accompany almost any meal, mid-course refresher, or snack.

YIELD: 1 QUART

1-1/2 cups	strawberry puree: (approximately 2 cups of whole strawberries, cleaned and hulled, in blender)	2/3 cup	water, cold
		1/3 cup	granulated sugar
		1 teaspoon	fresh lemon juice

In a small saucepan, combine the sugar and water and boil until the sugar is absorbed completely, to make a simple syrup. Combine all ingredients and churn in the bowl of an ice cream freezer for 20 to 25 minutes or until frozen. Pack into a covered container and place in the freezer until completely hardened. Garnish with strawberries and fresh mint leaves.

BAYONA
VANILLA ICE CREAM

YIELD: 1 QUART

2 cups	heavy cream
4 cups	half-and-half
1-1/2 cups	granulated sugar
10 large	egg yolks
1	vanilla bean, scraped

In a heavy-bottomed 2-quart saucepan, combine the cream, half-and-half, and scraped vanilla beans over low heat for approximately 10 minutes, stirring occasionally, to allow the flavors to infuse.

Increase the heat to high and watching carefully bring the mixture to just under a boil. Remove from heat and set aside. In a large bowl, whisk the yolks and sugar together until pale yellow. Temper the yolks by removing the pan from the heat and slowly drizzle approximately 1/4 cup hot cream into the yolks, whisking all the time, so the eggs do not scramble. Scrape the tempered yolk mixture back into the pan, return to the heat and cook, stirring constantly, until thickened. Quickly pour the mixture through a fine-mesh strainer into a clean container and set in an ice bath. Cool completely. Stir in the vanilla mixture and freeze in an ice cream maker according to the manufacturer's instructions.

ACCOMPANIMENTS GARNISHES & SAUCES

Decorations are not only for dessert anymore. The plate itself has become a stage for color and fanciful flourishes.

The dessert can loll about in a pool of coulis, which is a basic sweetened fruit puree, whipped cream, or crème anglaise. A squeeze bottle filled with either can be used to adorn serving plates with doodles, zigzags, squiggles, swirls, and polka dots. Use icings, meringue or whipped cream in a pastry bag that has been equipped with decorative tips. Ready-made meringue decorations are also available.

A small amount of practice on an empty plate will make your presentations look as spectacular as they taste. No matter how simple the dessert, presentation can elevate it to exquisite. A collection of serving pieces, glassware, ramekins, or bowls can be inexpensive or discovered in the most unlikely places in your kitchen cabinets.

Almost everyone in New Orleans has a patch of mint growing in a pot on the patio or under a leaky faucet in the back yard. Fresh mint, herbs, or small edible flowers such as pansies, violets, rose petals, or marigolds are also nature's colorful garnishes.

Chocolate curls are easily created by bringing a bar of chocolate to room temperature and shaving the edges with a potato peeler. Running an unsoftened chocolate bar down a cheese grater produces sweet crumbles. Dustings of sifted confectioners' sugar or cocoa and colored sugar crystals are punctuation marks across the dessert and plate that add eye appeal.

Brush grapes or berries with egg whites and roll them in granulated sugar to frost them and dress the plate or create a spectacular centerpiece for nibbling.

Sliced fruits and citrus twists or knots are colorful and a visual feast to cue the flavors or add a spark of color.

PRALINED PECANS

YIELD: 2 CUPS

2 cups	pecan halves, large
1/2 cup	granulated sugar
1/2 cup	dark brown sugar
2 tablespoons	unsalted butter, melted
1 tablespoon	light corn syrup

Preheat oven to 250°F.

Spread the pecans on a baking sheet. Place in the oven for 15 minutes to release the pecan's oils. Remove from oven and set aside.

Melt the butter in a medium skillet over a medium heat, and add the corn syrup. Add both sugars, stirring until all of the sugar has dissolved. Add pecans. Remove from heat and stir until the mixture thickens as it cools. Using tongs, remove each pecan from the warm sugar mixture. Place each pecan on a marble slab or piece of waxed paper and cool completely. They may be kept in a covered container for up to a week.

SWEET PECANS

YIELD: 2 CUPS

2 cups	pecan halves
1 tablespoon	granulated sugar
1/2 teaspoon	cinnamon
1 tablespoon	unsalted butter
pinch	salt

Preheat oven to 250°F.

Cover a baking sheet with baking parchment.

Melt the butter in skillet then add the sugar, cinnamon, and salt. Stir until all of the sugar has dissolved. Add the pecans, tossing gently in the sugar-butter mixture until evenly coated. Remove the pecans with a slotted spoon.

Spread pecans evenly on a parchment covered or greased baking sheet and place in the oven for 30 to 45 minutes, until golden brown and aromatic. Remove from oven and cool. They may be kept in a covered container for up to a week.

SPICY PECANS

YIELD: 2 CUPS

2 cups	pecan halves and pieces
2 tablespoons	unsalted butter, melted
1/2 teaspoon	cayenne pepper
1/2 teaspoon	black ground pepper
1/2 teaspoon	salt
dash	hot sauce (Tabasco®)

Preheat oven to 250°F.

Cover a baking sheet with baking parchment.

Melt the butter in skillet then add the peppers, hot sauce, and salt. Stir until the mixture is evenly distributed. Add the pecans, tossing gently until evenly coated. Remove the pecans with a slotted spoon.

Spread pecans evenly on a baking sheet and place in the oven for 30 to 45 minutes. Watch carefully until golden brown and aromatic. Remove from oven and cool. They may be kept in a covered container for up to a week or frozen in a zip lock bag for up to 3 months.

TOASTED PECANS

YIELD: 2 CUPS

2 cups   pecan halves and pieces

Chef Gary Darling, one of New Orleans famous Taste Buds, the trio of chef creators responsible for Semolina and Zea restaurants, taught me that toasting nuts allows them to release their oils, enhancing the flavor. It sounds simple, but who knew? Consequently, whenever we use nuts in almost any recipe we always follow Gary's excellent advice.

Preheat oven to 250°F.

Cover a baking sheet with baking parchment.

Spread pecans evenly on a baking sheet and place in the oven for 30 to 45 minutes. Watch carefully until golden brown and aromatic. Remove from oven and cool. They may be kept in a covered container for up to a week or frozen in a zip lock bag for up to 3 months.

Obviously this is not a complicated recipe, but it will make the nuts taste better and give them a little crunch.

CARAMEL SAUCE, EMERIL'S

YIELD: 3/4 CUP

3/4 cup	granulated sugar	1/2 cup	heavy whipping cream
2 tablespoons	water, cold		
1/2 teaspoon	fresh lemon juice	2 to 4 tablespoons	whole milk

In a medium heavy saucepan combine the sugar, water, and lemon juice. Cook over medium-high heat, stirring, until the sugar dissolves. Allow the liquid to boil without stirring until it becomes a deep amber color, 2 to 3 minutes, watching closely so it doesn't burn. Add the cream (be careful: it will bubble up), whisk to combine, and remove from the heat.

Stir in 2 tablespoons of the milk, then add more milk as necessary, up to 2 more tablespoons, until it has reached the consistency of syrup. The sauce will thicken as it cools. Warm sauce before serving.

CHOCOLATE BUTTER CREAM ICING

YIELD: 2 CUPS

2-1 ounce squares	unsweetened chocolate	1 cup	whole milk
		4 tablespoons	unsalted butter
2-1 ounce squares	semi-sweet chocolate	4 cups	confectioners' sugar

In the top of a double boiler, combine both chocolates, milk, and butter. Place over medium heat, and stir occasionally until the chocolate melts. Remove from the heat, and add the confectioners' sugar. Whisk with a fork until smooth. Refrigerate the icing for one hour to firm.

CHOCOLATE SAUCE, EMERIL'S

YIELD: 1 CUP

1/4 cup	half–and–half	1-1/3 cups	semi-sweet chocolate chips (1/2 pound)
1 tablespoon	unsalted butter		
		1/4 teaspoon	vanilla extract

In a small, heavy saucepan, combine the half-and-half, with the butter over medium heat until scalded. Remove from the heat.

Place the chocolate chips and vanilla extract in a medium, heatproof bowl. Add the half-and-half, and allow to stand for 2 minutes, then whisk until smooth.

Serve slightly warm. The sauce may be cooled to room temperature, and refrigerated in an airtight container for up to 3 days. Heat chocolate sauce slightly before serving.

CRÉME ANGLAISE

YIELD: 1 QUART

1 cup	heavy whipping cream
1 cup	half-and-half
1 whole	vanilla bean (split lengthwise and scrape seeds)
1/2 cup	granulated sugar
8 large	egg yolks

Place heavy whipping cream, half-and-half, and vanilla bean seeds on a medium heat until milk begins to simmer. If a more intense vanilla flavor is desired, also place the vanilla an husk into the cream. Whisk sugar and yolks together in bowl and very slowly add the hot cream into the eggs until the temperatures of each are equal. Place the eggs and sugar back into the pot and cook over low heat. This mixture will slowly thicken until it coats the back of a spoon. Strain, discard vanilla bean husk, and cover. Refrigerate crème anglaise.

TIP: To create a heart, spider web or other design, drop a bit of coulis on the surface of the crème anglaise and draw the tip of a knife across it in the direction that you want the color to move. Practice on an empty plate.

GRAHAM CRACKER CRUST, EMERIL'S

YIELD: 9-INCH PIE CRUST

1-1/4 cups	graham cracker crumbs
1/4 cup	granulated sugar
4 tablespoons	unsalted butter, melted

In a medium bowl, combine the graham cracker crumbs, and sugar, blended well. Add the butter, and use a fork to mix well. Press the mixture into the bottom and up the sides of a 9-inch pie pan. Top with a second pie pan, and with a circular motion, use it to press the crust firmly into the pan; remove the top pan.

Bake the crust blind (unfilled) using pie weights. Bake until browned, approximately 25 minutes. Allow the pie shell to cool completely.

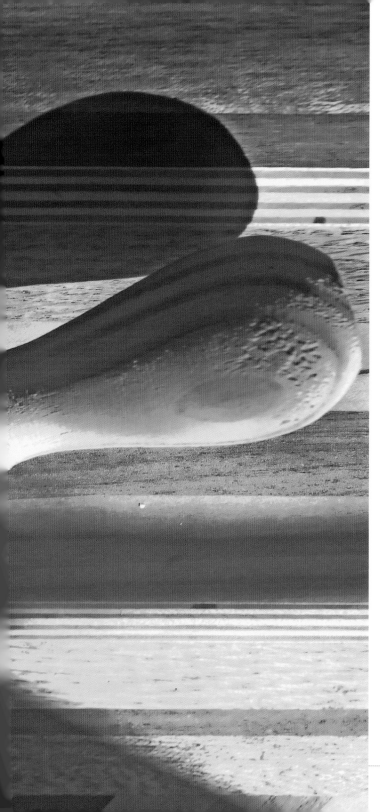

BAKING ESSENTIALS

Our pastry chef advisors emphasized that the proper tools and ingredients are essential. Consequently, the following are the items we collected and returned to most often to prepare these recipes. They will stir you to success.

Aluminum foil	Marble slab, 2- foot x 3- foot
Baker's Parchment	Matte knife
Baker's sugar, extra fine	Measuring cups set: dry
Baking powder	Measuring cups set: liquid
Baking sheets, best quality	Measuring spoons, two sets
Baking soda	Music
Butane kitchen torch	Oven-proof baking bags
Cake cooling racks	Paint brush, artist's small
Cake pans, 8" and 9", 2 to 4 of each	Pam spray, unflavored
Cake rounds, cardboard circles	Paper towels
Candy thermometer	Pastry bag with decorative tips
Cane Syrup	Pastry cutter
Cheese grater, small grate	Patience
Chinois	Pen, pencil
Chocolate, Baker's unsweetened	Pennies, pound
Chocolate, dark	Pie server
Chocolate, milk	Plastic binder for recipes & notes
Chocolate, semi-sweet	Plastic wrap
Chocolate, white	Pyrex pie pans
Cinnamon grated	Ramekins
Cinnamon sticks	Rolling Pin
Citrus peeler	Rubber spatulas, various sizes
Citrus zester	Ruler
Cocoa powder	Scissors
Colander	Serving dishes & platters, assortment
Condensed milk, sweetened	Sifter
Confectioners' sugar	Small bowls, assortment
Cookbook stand, acrylic	Spatula
Corn syrup, dark	Squeeze bottle, small tip
Corn syrup, light	Stainless steel mixing bowls:
Counter stand electric mixer	Storage containers with lids
Dry yeast	Strainer, small, medium & large mesh
Espresso powder	Sugar, brown
Evaporated milk	Sugar, light brown
Eye dropper	Tart tins
Fire extinguisher	Timer
Flour, all-purpose	Tongs, small and large
Flour, self-rising	Toothpicks, long
Glass mixing bowls, assortment	Unsalted butter
Granulated sugar	Vanilla, beans
Hand mixer, electric	Vanilla, pure extract, best quality
Icing spreader, crooked blade	Vegetable oil
Icing spreader, flat blade	Vegetable peeler
Kitchen Towels, 1 to 2 dozen	Waxed paper
Knife sharpener	Whisks, small, medium & large
Knives, assortment, excellent quality	Wooden chopping block
Ladles, small, medium & large	Wooden spoons, assortment

INDEX

ACKNOWLEDGEMENTS

A book occurs in the same way a recipe is prepared. A number of ingredients are carefully selected, prepared, and blended together to result in a sumptuous feast.

Talented people working together are the ingredients who brought New Orleans Classic Desserts to your table. They each made it happen, from busy restaurateurs and chefs to the wonderful staff at Pelican Publishing: Milburn and Nancy Calhoun, Nina Kooij, Amy Kirk, Terry Callaway, and Joseph Billingsley.

Chef April Bellow decoded restaurant recipes, tested, and retested them assisted by Eloisa Rivera. Pastry Chef Cathy Pollard offered her measure of expertise. Executive Chefs Robert Barker and Tommy DiGiovanni lent not only recipes but guidance, and explained some of the tricker aspects of confection cookery.

Real people in real home kitchens were the primary test cooks, people who have the usual odd assortment of equipment, just like you and me. Ginny Warren provided testing and insightful critiques from her expert tasting panel.

Delectable pages bring great desserts to life in all of their colorful, delicious glory. Photographers Rolfe Tessem, David Spielman, and Paul Rico directed me through new ways to see food through a view-finder.

Lloyd Dobyns, an acerbic journalist, lent his editing expertise, and observations. Brigit Binns, a top drawer professional, made certain that these recipes make sense. Michele Vine, a multi-talented Renaissance woman, backed me up in every aspect from food testing to editing and photography. They are each superb editors as well as authors in their own right. Any mistakes are mine, certainly not theirs. I'll try to answer any questions by e-mail to kit@neworleansclassicdesserts.com

My great thanks to Tom Fitzmorris, Susan Hennessey, Marie LeRuth, Tom Groom, Elise Abrams Antiques, Michael Nix, Casey Biggs, Megan Roen Forman, Marti Dalton, David Burrus, Jack Martzell, Robert Dabney, Jr., Colette Guste, Susan Spicer, Patty Fox, Mickey Caplinger, Perry Dolce, Charlie Dolce, Julie Smith, Bob Rintz, Linda Nix, Marc Leunissen, Kirbi Vine, Jane and Archie Casbarian, Sheila and Steve Bellaire, Michele Barker and Sule Lunat, Robin Blut, and Danielle Blut for their many contributions. Special thanks and love is owed to my patient family and friends.

Once again, Linda Ellerbee lifted my spirits with encouragement and laughter when none of the pieces fit and the cakes fell.